**PRACTICAL SCRIPTS FOR
EVERYDAY ENCOUNTERS**

OVERCOMING
SHYNESS

Other books by
Barbara Powell

**CAREERS FOR WOMEN AFTER MARRIAGE
AND CHILDREN**

HOW TO RAISE A SUCCESSFUL DAUGHTER

Barbara Powell, Ph.D.

PRACTICAL SCRIPTS FOR
EVERYDAY ENCOUNTERS

OVERCOMING
S H Y N E S S

McGraw-Hill Book Company

NEW YORK   ST. LOUIS   SAN FRANCISCO   AUCKLAND
BOGOTA   GUATEMALA   HAMBURG   JOHANNESBURG   LISBON
LONDON   MADRID   MEXICO   MONTREAL /NEW DELHI   PANAMA
PARIS   SAN JUAN   SÃO PAULO   SINGAPORE   SYDNEY
TOKYO   TORONTO

0317

Printed by
24 K Printing Co. Inc.
18 Acebo St. Marulas
Valenzuela, M. M.

*Reprinted under Authority
of Presidential Decree
No. 285 as amended by
P.D. Nos. 400 & 1203*

by

NATIONAL BOOK STORE INC.
701 Rizal Avenue Cor. Soler
Tel. Nos. 49-43-06 to 09

REPRINTED & EXCLUSIVELY DISTRIBUTED BY:

First paperback edition, 1981

LIBRARY OF CONGRESS CATALOGING IN PUBLICATION DATA
Powell, Barbara, date
  Overcoming shyness.
  Includes index.
  1. Bashfulness.   I. Title.
BF575.B3P63   158'.2   79-12609

ISBN 971-08-3007-4

Book design by Roberta Rezk

To my shy clients

Acknowledgments

I would like to express my gratitude to my literary agent, Lisa Collier, for her original suggestions on this project; to Robert D. Armstrong for giving me the benefit of his experience as an executive recruiter and his thoughtful assistance in preparing the chapter on overcoming shyness on the job; and to my daughter, Julie O'Neill, for her invaluable help in typing and proofreading the manuscript.

CONTENTS

Part

WHAT'S
THE
PROBLEM

How do You Know 1 if you're Shy?

How do you know if you're shy?

If you have to ask, you're probably not shy, or in any case not *very* shy. Almost everyone feels shy on some occasions, with certain people, or at certain times of life. If you went through a shy period and came out of it, it's most likely that period was adolescence.

Shyness means different things to different people. Timid, bashful, quiet, unassuming, reserved—these are all words used at times to describe shy people. But shyness isn't necessarily the same as being quiet. Some people are naturally quiet and reserved, while others are very gregarious and outgoing. Shyness generally means feeling tongue-tied, awkward, and self-conscious in social situations.

Usually a degree of physical discomfort—a fast heartbeat, nervous stomach, clammy hands, perspiration, weak knees, or feelings of lightheadedness or dizziness—accompany the subjective feelings of awkwardness. These are the same symptoms experienced in other anxiety states and phobic conditions. One other symptom, blushing, seems uniquely related to feelings of shyness or social embarrassment.

I suppose it is possible to feel shy without experiencing any physical discomfort, but I have never encountered an extremely shy person who didn't feel some anxiety symptoms. However, shyness doesn't always involve a conversational deficit. Some shy people react to their anxiety not by being tongue-tied but by talking too much. I have also worked with clients who lacked any outward sign of shyness: they could make conversation easily in virtually any situation, but inwardly they felt tense, anxious, fluttery, and extremely uncomfortable.

My definition of a shy person, for the purpose of this book, is an individual who consistently has difficulty making conversation with others or experiences severe physical symptoms of anxiety in social situations or, as is most frequently the case, has both of these problems.

Most shy people are also nonassertive—they have difficulty speaking up for themselves. But it is certainly possible to be nonassertive without being shy. Shy people are usually at a loss for words. Nonassertive people are at a loss for *certain* words such as "No," "I want," "I like," and "I disagree." Both shy people and nonassertive people tend to be low on self-confidence. Becoming less shy, or more assertive, or both, will help you be more self-confident and feel better about yourself.

Shyness is most likely to overtake you when you are entering a new phase of life, like adolescence, or are trying to make a new circle of friends after a divorce or after moving to a new city. You may also feel especially shy in unfamiliar situations, such as unexpectedly finding yourself seated next to a celebrity at a dinner party.

You may be surprised to learn that some of these celebrities are shy themselves. Barbara Walters, the most highly paid woman in television, comments, "I have a slight inferiority complex still. I go into a room and have to talk myself into going up to people. . . . I can't take a vacation alone, eat in a restaurant alone, have cocktails alone." And Walters' successor on the *Today* show, Jane Pauley, remarked when she was visiting my first Shyness Clinic at the University of Connecticut that she could never do what I was trying to teach my students that day: go up and introduce themselves to a group of two or three strangers at a party.

Tennessee Williams relates: "I remember the occasion on which my constant blushing had its beginning. I believe it was in a class in plane geometry. I happened to look across the aisle and a dark and attractive girl was looking directly into my eyes and at once I felt my face burning. It burned more and more intensely after I had faced front again. My God, I thought, I'm blushing because she looked into my eyes or I into hers and suppose this happens whenever my eyes look into the eyes of another? . . . As soon as I had entertained that nightmarish speculation, it was immediately turned into a reality. . . . Literally, from that incident on, and almost without remission for the next four or five years, I would blush whenever a pair of human eyes, male or female, would meet mine."

Catherine Drinker Bowen, author of many best-selling biographies, recalled in *Family Portrait:*

> The pains my mother took on occasion to declare that people liked me must have been due to the fact that I was at the time quite bitterly shy. Small wonder my diary at eleven declared that I would die without Mamma. "It is a terrible misfortune to be born shy," I wrote just after my

twelfth birthday, in a thick school notebook labeled *Vol. 3*, *dedicated to Mamma*. "You can't talk to anybody because you don't know what to say. You get embarrassed all the more if you don't talk and altogether it is a *terrible* mick-sup to be shy and tonguetied when you are with strangers. I would love and adore to be popular.... There is little doubt that what made me so shy was a consciousness of my looks...." The diary spoke often of shyness and lined up the enemy in categories: "I don't mind old gentlemen, above 45. I don't mind old ladies, above 45. I don't mind young ladies under 30 much. I *do* mind young gentlemen under 30."

And Mark Twain, asked by a New York reporter, just prior to his departure for London in 1907, who were the people who had come to see him off, replied, "Oh, I do not know. The fact is, I am the shyest person you ever saw. Most people are shy, but mine is of a peculiar sort. I never look people in the face, because they may know me and I do not know them. And that is so embarrassing."

Those are just a few examples of well-known people who are, or were, shy. Shyness occurs in people of all ages and all social backgrounds. Some people appear shy because they are self-conscious about some aspect of their appearance or personality. One patient I was recently seeing for a lifelong obesity problem admitted that when he was a teen-ager his mother had to hold his hand while he phoned a girl to ask for a date. Another overweight and very shy patient, after seeing a photograph of one of my groups of shy students in *The New York Times*, commented, "I was surprised by the way they looked. I thought they must all be shy because they were fat and ugly. But they were all very attractive people."

Philip Zimbardo, who has done a great deal of research

on shyness, surveyed more than 5000 people and found that 80 percent had considered themselves shy at one time, while 40 percent currently felt shy. One fourth of those surveyed were "chronically shy" and 4 percent felt shy *all* the time, in all situations. Only 7 percent said they had never felt shy.

Of those who considered themselves shy, 80 percent felt reluctant to talk in social situations and half had difficulty with eye contact. Eighty-five percent were excessively preoccupied with themselves, concerned with what others would think of them, and worried about being inadequate, ugly, or stupid.

Other studies have found that firstborns are more likely to be shy, and that shy children usually have a poor self-image and feel they are too tall, too fat, weak, stupid, or unpopular. In a University of California study of 252 children, more girls than boys were shy at all ages and shyness in children seemed to be related to shyness in parents.

My own research and clinical experience suggests that a majority of shy people had at least one shy parent. Most of the shy people I have encountered recall being frequently criticized or ridiculed as children, either by their parents, teachers, or peers, or were subjected to very high levels of parental expectations. "My father was a perfectionist," one woman declared. "I had to do things over and over until they met his standards. My parents never gave encouragement or approval, and I always felt there was something lacking within myself." Another commented, "My parents continually criticized my weight (I was too thin), my eating habits, and my attempts to do housework. They never paid attention to me unless some problem existed." A third recalled, "My mother was extremely critical of the way I looked, dressed, and behaved. My father never criticized me, but he rarely interfered with my mother's highly emotional attacks on the way I looked and my wicked character. I always felt I was a very inferior person."

The traumatic effects of peer ridicule were expressed by a fifty-three-year-old woman who had worn hand-me-down clothes as a child: "I was frequently ridiculed by other children for my clothing, which was serviceable but not fashionable and very *outdated*. I was always trying to stay out of sight. Though I did well enough in school, as time went on I didn't care any more about grades. I hated to be called on in class even if I knew the answers. I had too many embarrassing moments to list. It seemed a part of my childhood."

Some shy people recall an especially painful or embarrassing event that either made them shy or reinforced their shyness. One woman remembered "blanking out" on stage during a spelling bee and misspelling a word she knew well. Another said, "A fellow student imitated my walk in class, when the teacher was out of the room." A businessman vividly remembered the day in first grade when he wet his pants in class because he was afraid to hold up his hand and ask permission to go to the bathroom.

The single feature I have found most often in the background of shy people is a poor self-image during childhood. These individuals regarded themselves as too thin, too fat, too small, too large, or otherwise different. Quite a few wore glasses at an early age. Being clumsy at sports was a difficulty for some; a more frequent memory is "feeling stupid" but (for girls at least) being "too smart" could also produce feelings of unpopularity. Whether these deficiencies were real or imagined, they caused the individual to feel different, self-conscious, and shy. If you are shy, you may very well recall some feeling of being different from others as a child.

But even though the roots of shyness go back to childhood or adolescence, you don't have to continue being shy if you don't want to. (Philip Zimbardo's research indicates that between 10 and 20 percent of those who say they are shy *like* being that way.)

If you like it, fine! I'm certainly not going to try and convince you that you should change. But I have never come across a severely shy person who liked being that way. If your shyness is a source of discomfort to you, I would like to help you change—and you can change if you really want to.

Recently a client of mine, a young woman in her twenties, commented, "I'm just getting used to the idea that I really can change, and it's exciting. I used to excuse or accept certain things that I did but didn't like by saying 'That's just the way I am.' Now I realize I don't have to be that way if I don't want to."

A gestalt therapist told me the other day that she had encouraged a patient to "get in touch with your shyness—just experience it, walk into a party, don't worry about talking to people—just get in touch with being shy." I don't agree with this approach at all. I think it is more important to *change* behavior that is bothering you than to get in touch with it. And I think you can change if shyness is a real problem for you.

I have found through experience that shyness can be treated very effectively through a combination of procedures that work well either individually or in groups. Since these procedures are quite simple, there is no reason you can't use them on your own to overcome your shyness problem.

If you have a vivid imagination—and most shy people do, since they tend to spend a good deal of time in fantasy—the techniques will be easier for you to apply. Imaginary rehearsals (vividly visualizing yourself in different situations) are one key aspect of my treatment approach. You've probably already been doing this, just to get away from it all, for some time. Now you will be using your imagination to help you overcome your shyness problem.

To derive the fullest benefit from your imaginary rehearsals, you must be completely relaxed. I have never yet had a client who couldn't relax sufficiently to profit from this procedure. I will give you step-by-step instructions to help you relax physically.

Of course, you can't conquer this problem by imagination alone. You must practice. I give my students and clients specific behavioral assignments to carry out between sessions or group meetings, after they have rehearsed the situations in their imaginations and also with me or with other group members. If you are trying to overcome shyness on your own, you will have to work out your own behavioral assignments.

Since many shy people have not developed the conversational skill they need in social situations, I have provided sample scripts to help you in your imaginary rehearsals and subsequently in real-life situations. Of course, when you become more self-confident and more adept at conversation you will no longer need my scripts but will spontaneously create your own.

Before you start tackling your shyness, take my Shyness Quiz and compare your reactions with those of the typical client I treat for shyness.

SHYNESS QUIZ

I. Circle the most appropriate number on a scale of 0 to 10, where 0 = not at all shy and 10 = extremely shy:

How shy do you consider
yourself?   0 1 2 3 4 5 6 7 8 9 10

II. Shy people frequently experience discomfort in the six situations described below. Indicate, by circling the most appropriate numbers, the degree to which you currently experience these feelings and reactions in each situation. Then add up the numbers you have circled for all six situations.

Situation One

You are in a one-to-one situation with a person of the same sex—someone you don't know well but would like to know better.

	NOT AT ALL	VERY MUCH

1. I avoid this situation.   0 1 (2) 3 4 5 6 7 8 9 10

When in this situation:

2. I am extremely tense.   0 1 (2) 3 4 5 6 7 8 9 10
3. I feel tongue-tied: can think of nothing to say, or the words come out wrong.   0 1 (2) 3 4 5 6 7 8 9 10
4. I have one or more of the following symptoms: profuse perspiration, nervous stomach, fast heart rate, or blushing.   0 1 (2) 3 4 5 6 7 8 9 10
5. I have sometimes felt so panicky that I had to get up and leave.   0 1 (2) 3 4 5 6 7 8 9 10

Situation Two

You are in a one-to-one situation with a person of the opposite sex—someone you don't know well but would like to know better.

1. I avoid this situation.   0 1 2 3 4 5 6 7 8 9 10

When in this situation:

2. I am extremely tense.   0 1 2 3 4 5 6 7 8 9 10
3. I feel tongue-tied: can think of nothing to say, or the words come out wrong.   0 1 2 3 4 5 6 7 8 9 10
4. I have one or more of the following symptoms: profuse perspiration, nervous stomach, fast heart rate, or blushing.   0 1 2 3 4 5 6 7 8 9 10
5. I have sometimes felt so panicky that I had to get up and leave.   0 1 2 3 4 5 6 7 8 9 10

Situation Three

You are in a one-to-one situation with a well-known person

or an authority figure and feel you must make conversation for a few minutes.

	NOT AT ALL	VERY MUCH
1. I avoid this situation.	0 1 2 3 4 5 6 7 8 ⑨ 10

When in this situation:

2. I am extremely tense.   0 1 2 3 4 5 6 7 8 ⑨ 10
3. I feel tongue-tied: can think of nothing to say, or the words come out wrong.   0 1 2 3 4 5 6 7 8 9 10
4. I have one or more of the following symptoms: profuse perspiration, nervous stomach, fast heart rate, or blushing.   0 1 2 3 4 5 6 ⑦ 8 9 10
5. I have sometimes felt so panicky that I had to get up and leave.   0 1 2 3 4 5 6 ⑦ 8 9 10

SITUATION FOUR

You are being interviewed for a job you want.

1. I avoid this situation.   0 1 2 3 4 5 6 7 8 ⑨ 10

When in this situation:

2. I am extremely tense.   0 1 2 3 4 5 6 7 8 9 10
3. I feel tongue-tied: can think of nothing to say, or the words come out wrong.   0 1 2 3 4 5 6 7 8 9 10
4. I have one or more of the following symptoms: profuse perspiration, nervous stomach, fast heart rate, or blushing.   0 1 2 3 4 ⑤ 6 7 8 9 10
5. I have sometimes felt so panicky that I had to get up and leave.   0 1 2 ③ 4 5 6 7 8 9 10

SITUATION FIVE

You are in a class, seminar, or business meeting where you are required or expected to participate by asking and answering questions.

1. I avoid this situation.   0 1 2 3 4 5 6 7 8 ⑨ 10

When in this situation:

NOT AT ALL　　VERY MUCH

2. I am extremely tense.　　0 1 2 3 4 5 6 7 8 9 10
3. I feel tongue-tied: can think of nothing to say, or the words come out wrong.　　0 1 2 3 4 5 6 7 8 9 10
4. I have one or more of the following symptoms: profuse perspiration, nervous stomach, fast heart rate, or blushing.　　0 1 2 3 4 5·6 7 8 9 10
5. I have sometimes felt so panicky that I had to get up and leave.　　0 1 2 3 4 5 6 7 8 9 10

SITUATION SIX

You are at a party or some other social situation where you do not know anyone very well.

1. I avoid this situation.　　0 1 2 3 4 5 6 7 8 9 10

When in this situation:

2. I am extremely tense.　　0 1 2 3 4 5 6 7 8 9 10
3. I feel tongue-tied: can think of nothing to say, or the words come out wrong.　　0 1 2 3 4 5 6 7 8 9 10
4. I have one or more of the following symptoms: profuse perspiration, nervous stomach, fast heart rate, or blushing.　　0 1 2 3 4 5 6 7 8 9 10
5. I have sometimes felt so panicky that I had to get up and leave.　　0 1 2 3 4 5 6 7 8 9 10

Most severely shy people rate themselves five or above on the question "How shy do you consider yourself?" and have a total score of 75 or more for the six situations. Of course, some people feel very concerned about shyness even though their scores total less than 75. If you consider shyness a problem for you, you can help yourself by using the techniques you will learn by reading this book.

Sizing Up 2 your Shyness

In the next chapter I'm going to give you detailed instructions for the relaxation procedure that will enable you to carry out the imaginary rehearsals I will describe in this book (as well as others you create for yourself to help you overcome difficulties in situations I don't cover specifically). It will be very important for you to follow the relaxation instructions exactly to obtain the greatest benefits from your rehearsals.

In the meantime, let's carry out your first imaginary experience in a more informal way.

First, imagine that you are consulting me as a client to obtain help in overcoming your shyness.

Perhaps you feel that you just wouldn't consult a psychologist about shyness. Maybe you feel the problem isn't serious enough, or that going to a psychologist means you're "crazy," or that you'd simply be too shy to make the initial phone call or to tell me about your problem once you arrived at my office. But the fact that you are reading this book does indicate that you are seeking help in overcoming your problem.

So let's go a step beyond reading about shyness and imagine that you are here in my office discussing the problem with me. Because you are so bothered by your shyness, you have overcome your initial fear sufficiently to make an appointment. The time for your appointment has arrived, and you are sitting in my small reception room waiting for the client ahead of you to depart. The chances are you will be feeling rather nervous about the prospects of discussing your shyness with someone you don't know. You may never have talked about it with anyone before. You may never have even allowed yourself to think about it in the way you are going to be thinking about it now.

Most people find that the informal atmosphere of my reception room and office, a former sunroom with windows opening onto a vista of trees and sky, helps to put them at ease.

Nevertheless, as you sit there waiting you are probably feeling nervous. If so, your thoughts and feelings are very similar to those of most clients who are seeing a psychiatrist, psychologist, or other therapist for the first time. It isn't easy to unburden yourself to a stranger. In many cases, it's a stranger you know very little about. While some clients are referred by physicians, school psychologists, or other professionals, many simply pick up the telephone directory and select a name from the yellow pages.

Since you are consulting me now—not last month or next month, but right now—there's a good chance that something has recently occurred to convince you that you must get help with your problem. You may be facing a job change, or you may be new to the community and feeling isolated, or you may have just had your thirtieth birthday and realized that life seems to be passing you by. The list of possible *ors* is endless, but for some reason you feel you can't live with your problem any longer. You've decided to take action.

Whatever the reason for your decision, it's relatively certain that you are wondering not only what I am going to be like, but also what the interview itself will be like, and what you are going to say and feel.

In the first interview I take a careful history, try to size up the problem and give the client some idea of how I will try to help him or her overcome it. That is what I am also hoping to accomplish in this chapter. So let's assume that you are in my office now, telling me about your shyness problem.

It could be that you'll begin by saying "I don't know where to start." Clients often do begin that way.

In that case, I'll try to help out by asking a few questions.

"How long has shyness been a problem for you? Can you remember exactly when it started?" Jane, a woman in her thirties completing a business school program, consulted me for a severe speech phobia that caused her untold anxiety in every interview, every class where she was likely to be called on, and in every other situation where her statements might be questioned or she might have to defend herself. She came because she was nearing the end of her degree program and would soon be scheduling job interviews.

Careful questioning revealed that Jane had not always been shy. At age eighteen, she was raped. Charges were brought against the offender and Jane recalls the courtroom scene as almost more traumatic than the crime itself. The attorneys defending the rapist attacked and ridiculed her statements, and the finding was "not guilty."

This experience was so painful for Jane that she had almost succeeded in repressing it and had never made the seemingly obvious connection between her present anxieties in evaluative situations and the courtroom trauma. I wish I could report that the mere recall of this episode was sufficient to dissipate Jane's anxieties, but things did not—and seldom do—work out that way. However, Jane succeeded in reducing her anxieties to manageable levels so that she could cope with interviews and seminars by relaxing physically, applying imaginary rehearsal techniques, and by changing the way she talked to herself.

Of course, most shyness problems do not have such dramatic onsets, but I want you to recall everything you can about the origin of your shyness.

And I want to know why you are seeking help for the problem *now*. What has happened recently that has made you feel you must do something about being shy? One woman lawyer recently consulted me because she had just had the second of two unsuccessful job interviews. She was told by the lawyers who interviewed her on both occasions that while they were sure she could handle the legal aspects of the job, she came across as too quiet and unassuming to be effective in the interpersonal relationships involved.

What are the physical manifestations of your shyness, and how severe are they? Do you suffer from clammy hands, a pounding heart, nervous stomach, frequency of urination, weak knees, dizziness, blushing, or some combination of these—or some other symptom I haven't mentioned?

Some people are more concerned about the physical symptoms than about the emotions that provoke them. A young man recently flew halfway across the country to consult me because, though he had no difficulty in making conversation, he found himself embarrassingly drenched in perspiration in crowds or when with even one other person he did not know well. He had no control over his symptom and was becoming increasingly concerned about it. A priest came because his hands shook so noticeably while serving communion that parishioners frequently inquired why he was so nervous.

Another client, a woman in her fifties, was so embarrassed by her constant blushing that she sought help in overcoming it, even though she did not consider herself shy. But careful questioning on my part, and careful record-keeping on hers, revealed the fact that her blushing always occurred in situations in which she felt inferior educationally or socially. The wife of a successful merchant, this woman was an attractive and charming person but was extremely conscious of her limited cultural background and her lack of a college education. She lived in a wealthy upper-middle-class suburb.

Blushing is almost always a source of extreme embarrassment to those who experience it, and some people actually avoid many social situations because they are afraid of blushing. When I first encountered this problem, I looked in vain in psychological and psychiatric journals for information about the treatment of blushing, and concluded that either no one had sought help for blushing in the recent past or that the therapists they consulted had not been able to effect a cure. But after some unsuccessful experiences myself in attempting to treat blushing directly by means of temperature training (a kind of biofeedback), I realized that blushing has to be treated indirectly by reducing anxiety in the situations that lead to blushing.

Therefore, while I want to know exactly what physical symptoms you experience in social situations, the objective of treatment will be to reduce your anxiety in these situations, and thus indirectly reduce the physical manifestations.

My experience in working with shy people leads me to believe that most people suffering from shyness—and they do suffer!—actually have two difficulties. First, they are extremely tense in social situations. Second, they lack certain social skills and do not know what to do or say in some situations. This adds to their existing anxieties or creates new ones.

This is why, in addition to using relaxation and imagination to allay anxieties, and helping people find more positive ways of talking to themselves and thinking about themselves, I teach clients what to say and do in the situations in which they feel uncomfortable.

One of my clients, a cashier who dealt with many of the same customers day after day, was so shy that she experienced great difficulty in calling her customers by name. I had her imagine herself doing this over and over again, and had her practice saying in my office "Good morning, Mr. Jones. . . . Hello, Mrs. Smith. . . . Isn't it a nice day, Miss White?" The next week she related a dream in which she was in a classroom with a group of very young children. They were seated in children's chairs and she was the only adult. The chair was too small for her, of course. I was the teacher and was standing in front of the class drilling them in saying "Good morning, Mr. Jones. . . . Good afternoon, Mrs. Jones." Her dream seemed to express her feeling that she was only now learning a skill that most people acquired at a much earlier age.

Why some people learn and others don't is not entirely clear. This particular client had parents who were not very talkative themselves and failed to teach her some basic verbal skills. Not only did they fail to teach her, but their own behavior failed to provide her with the opportunity to observe normal social interaction. Some of our most important learning occurs through observing the way others, most often our parents, behave. I'm sure that is why so many shy parents produce shy children.

Before I ask you to make a detailed analysis of the situations in which you feel shy, I want to define a term we will be using from time to time: *desensitization.* When I talk about imaginary rehearsals under relaxed conditions, I am actually talking about desensitization.

Basically the word means just what logic would tell you: to remove sensitivity. Allergists use the term for describing a series of shots to neutralize a person's reaction to a certain substance or event—bee stings, for example. Psychologists use the word to refer to a particular procedure first described in 1958 by Joseph Wolpe, a Philadelphia psychiatrist who came to this country from South Africa.

Wolpe discovered that phobic patients could overcome their fears if they imagined themselves in the feared situations while in a state of relaxation. Desensitization therefore involves two basic elements: relaxation and a list or hierarchy of feared situations, beginning with the least feared and proceeding to the most feared, which the patient imagines while in a relaxed state. The hierarchy of situations is developed before the actual desensitization is started. While the hierarchy is being worked out, the patient is also being trained in relaxation.

For a patient with a fear of heights, the first item on the hierarchy might be "standing on the lowest rung of a ladder," while the last might be "going to the top of the Empire State Building."

A hierarchy is created by having the patient list all anxiety-producing situations, then arrange them in ascending order. Wolpe has patients rate situations on a scale of 0 to 100, 0 representing a state of perfect calm, 100 being panic.

Though the ratings are entirely subjective, they allow client and therapist to get a clear idea of the relative anxiety experienced in different situations.

Obviously, an individual may feel anxiety in a variety of different settings. A person may fear heights and enclosed spaces as well as interpersonal situations. In such cases separate hierarchies, as many as necessary, may be developed.

Since Wolpe's original work, virtually every imaginable fear has been treated by desensitization. While the results are not perfect every time, the procedure is usually very helpful.

I'd like to teach you how to desensitize yourself to your interpersonal anxieties. The first step is to create a hierarchy of situations which bother you.

Begin by rating the situations covered in Chapters 5 through 12, using a scale of 0 to 100, where 0 = perfect calm and 100 = panic or near-panic. These scenes include those I have found most frequently to cause anxiety for shy clients. Some of them will not cause you to feel anxious; others will not apply to you, so rate only those situations that do apply and do cause you to feel anxious.

The easiest way to set up your hierarchy is to list each scene (Chapter 5, Act II, Scene 3, page 66, for example) on a separate index card and then arrange the cards in order of your ratings. After you have done this, you may find that you need to re-evaluate some of your ratings. If you rated "introducing yourself to a fellow student" 50 and "asking a classmate for a date" 50, you should ask yourself if both of these situations actually arouse exactly the same degree of anxiety.

Ideally, your shyness hierarchy should include situations ranging from a low of about 10 to a high of 95 or 100, representing the most anxious you have ever felt in a social situation.

And, also ideally, you should have steps that are not too far apart in the amount of anxiety they produce. If your lowest scene is rated 10, your next should be no higher than 20. You may need to think of additional scenes or situations to fill in the intermediate steps.

After you have started desensitizing yourself to your social anxieties, you may think of additional scenes to include in your hierarchy. You can simply write them out on separate index cards, rate them, and insert them at the appropriate place in your deck of cards.

By this time you should have made a great deal of progress in sizing up your shyness. You've determined which situations make you anxious and exactly how anxious each situation makes you.

Now you are ready to do something about it.

Part **2**

DOING SOMETHING ABOUT IT

How to Conduct 3 a Rehearsal: Relax and Imagine It

First of all, you are going to need a cassette tape recorder, preferably one that shuts off automatically.

If you don't already own or have convenient access to a tape recorder, there are several good models on the market in the thirty- to fifty-dollar price bracket. (Don't buy the least expensive one you can find, or you may end up in the same position as one client who did just that, and then had to purchase another because the first was so noisy she couldn't relax while listening to it.)

Try out the machine or a demonstration model before you buy it to make certain that operating noise is not excessive, and buy it from a reliable store in case you discover when you get home that your machine doesn't sound like the one in the store. And save the original wrappings until you are satisfied that the recorder does not have to be returned.

You will need a sixty-minute tape (thirty minutes on each side).

While you may be tempted to skip the tape recorder and try to follow the relaxation instructions straight from the book, don't. After experience with hundreds of clients, some using taped relaxation instructions and some following the same procedure without taped instructions, I can state emphatically that I have *never* seen a client find the relaxation procedure as beneficial without a tape as with one.

I'm not sure exactly why. Part of the difference, I think, is that taped instructions provide a uniform pace for the exercise. Without a tape, most clients go through the exercise too quickly—and lose much of the benefit. I have tried relaxation myself both with and without a tape, and find the tape much more effective.

Another factor may be that the voice provides a focal attention point, which aids in the relaxation process.

Your tape recorder, then, will provide the audio aid needed for your relaxation practice. You will also need a visual aid, but this is something you will create out of your own imagination and memory.

To do this, think of the most relaxing scene you have ever experienced, and paint a picture of it in your mind just as vividly as you can. You may want to recreate a beach you have visited, a place in the mountains or the forest where you have felt especially peaceful and relaxed on a camping trip. Your scene should be one that has a great deal of meaning for you. I recall one client who preferred to visualize lying in her bed at home, surrounded by pillows and reading a novel. Another liked to think of herself reclining in a lawn chair in her backyard. A student living away from home felt most relaxed visualizing himself in a particular armchair in his family's home, listening to a favorite record.

But the beach remains the most popular choice. I have had beaches in Nantucket, Hawaii, Florida, California, and Norwalk, Connecticut, described to me. If the idea of sand and sea means relaxation to you, paint a mental picture of a specific beach. Imagine the color of the sky and the water, the warmth of the sun, the feel of the sand under your body and the soft breeze against your face, and hear the waves lapping gently on the shore.

Now that you have selected your relaxing image, write out a brief paragraph that will help you visualize it clearly. (You may find, after trying it out, that your scene evokes some painful or stressful memories. If so, look for another scene.) Your paragraph should follow this approximate format (Copy B), adding whatever additional specific details occur to you.

COPY B: *"Now that you are so relaxed,* you can relax even further by visualizing yourself at that beautiful beach on [Nantucket, Hawaii, etc.] where you feel so calm and so relaxed. Visualize very clearly the vivid blue sky with its fleecy white clouds, and the endless stretch of serene blue water as you look out to sea. Feel the warmth of the afternoon sun on your body and the warm, grainy sand against your skin. Enjoy the gentle sound of the waves against the beach and the distant laughter of children as they play in the water. Enjoy the feeling of calm and relaxation that comes over you. Say to yourself 'I feel calm and relaxed . . . peaceful and relaxed.' "

When you have written the relaxing scene to your satisfaction, with as much concrete detail as possible, you are ready to begin experimenting with your tape recorder, if you haven't done so already.

Before making the final tape, which you will be working with for the next few days or weeks, you will want to do some practice work to familiarize yourself with the recorder and with the sound of your own voice. (None of my shy clients started off with any great familiarity with tape recorders, and I am assuming this will also be the case with you.) Many people are surprised when they first hear their voice on tape. You will need to get over this initial reaction, which may well be one of displeasure ("Do I sound like *that?*"), before you can start using the tape recorder therapeutically. So practice speaking into the microphone (even if your machine will record without a microphone, you are better off using one; extraneous noise will be greatly reduced) and modify the tone of your voice until you are satisfied. Try for a slow, soothing monotone. You are after a pleasant, relaxing effect, not drama. If listening to your voice makes you feel sleepy, you are on the right track.

The paragraph you have written describing your relaxing scene will be good practice material for your first recording sessions, since it will be a part of your final tape.

As soon as you are comfortable with your tape recorder and with your recording voice, read over Copy A (page 29) and Copy C (page 33) to become acquainted with the content.

At this point you are ready to record. It may be necessary to make several attempts before you achieve a recording that satisfies you. An inadvertent cough or the ringing of a telephone or doorbell may be recorded and require a fresh start.

To minimize the likelihood of these distractions, sit in a comfortable chair in a quiet room with the doors closed and the telephone off the hook. Take any other precautions you can think of to insure that you will not be disturbed.

Since this is the first of two recordings you will be making, I'm going to refer to it as Side 1.

Recording Side 1

Allow the recorder to run for a few seconds before you begin recording Copy A; otherwise the first few words may be lost. Record Copy A as indicated, then your own tailor-made Copy B, followed by Copy C.

COPY A: Settle back as comfortably as you can. Close your eyes and just let yourself relax completely now.

Begin by concentrating on the muscles in your hands ... clench your fists tightly and study that feeling of tension. [*Pause for five seconds.*] Now slowly relax your hands ... just let all of the tension flow out. Go on relaxing them all the way, and notice the feeling of relaxation. [*Pause for five seconds.*] Once more, clench your fists and study that feeling of tension. [*Pause for five seconds.*] Now, very slowly, relax those muscles again. Just let your hands relax completely. . . . You may feel a tingling sensation in your hands as you allow them to relax more and more . . . .

Now that your hands are relaxed like that, tense the muscles in your upper arms—just the upper arms. Keep your hands relaxed. Feel the tension [*Pause for five seconds*] ... and now, very slowly, let your arms relax completely. Notice the difference between the feeling of tension and the feeling of relaxation. . . . Once more, tense the muscles in your upper arms and hold the tension for a few seconds [*Pause for five seconds*] ... and now, relax those muscles again. Relax them all the way. Your hands and arms should be feeling completely relaxed now.

Now that your hands and arms are relaxed like that, tense the muscles in your forehead by raising your eyebrows. Study that feeling of tension and hold it for a few seconds. [*Pause for five seconds.*] ... Now, very slowly and gradually, release all of that tension. Just let those muscles relax completely, and enjoy the very pleasant contrast between the feeling of tension and the feeling of relaxation. [*Pause for five seconds.*] Once more, tense those muscles in your forehead [*Pause for five seconds*] . . . and now, very slowly, relax them again. Just go on relaxing them all the way. . . .

Now that your forehead is relaxed like that, tense the muscles in your eyes by closing them very tightly. [*Pause for five seconds.*] Now, very slowly and gradually, relax those muscles, and notice the difference between the feeling of tension and the feeling of relaxation. . . . Once more, tense those muscles in your eyes by closing them tightly [*Pause for five seconds*] . . . and now relax them again, very slowly and gradually.

Now that your forehead and your eyes are feeling so relaxed, concentrate your attention on the muscles in your nose. Tense those by wrinkling up the skin on your nose, and hold the tension for a few minutes. [*Pause for five seconds.*] Now, very slowly, let those muscles relax completely. Notice the difference between the feeling of tension and the feeling of relaxation. . . . Once more, tense those muscles in your nose [*Pause for five seconds*] . . . and now relax them again. Just go on relaxing them all the way. . . .

Now that the upper part of your face is relaxed like that, tense the muscles in your lips by grinning very broadly, and study the feeling of tension in your lips and in your jaws. [*Pause for five seconds.*] Now, very slowly and gradually, let all of that tension flow out. Enjoy the pleasing contrast between the feeling of tension and the feeling of relaxation. [*Pause for five seconds.*] Once more, tense up those muscles in your mouth [*Pause for five seconds*] . . . and now, very slowly, relax the muscles again, letting your mouth return to a natural resting position with the lips slightly parted. [*Pause for five seconds.*]

Now your entire face is feeling very relaxed, very pleasantly relaxed. . . . Tense the muscles in your chin by pressing down on an imaginary book. Study the tension that you feel in your chin, in your jaws, and in the back of your neck. [*Pause for five seconds.*] Very slowly now, relax those muscles completely . . . just let all the tension flow out. Go on relaxing those muscles as much as you possibly can. Enjoy the pleasant contrast between the feeling of tension and the feeling of relaxation. . . . Once more, tense those muscles by pressing down on an imaginary book, and hold the tension for a few seconds. [*Pause for five seconds.*] . . . Now, very slowly and gradually, relax the muscles again. Just enjoy those very pleasant, relaxing feelings. Now your entire face and neck are feeling very relaxed, calm and relaxed. . . .

Tense the muscles in your shoulders now by pulling your shoulders forward and together. Hold that tension for a few seconds . . . be very aware of it. [*Pause for five seconds.*] And now, very slowly, let all those muscles relax . . . just let them relax completely, all the way. Notice the very pleasant difference between the feeling of tension and the feeling of relaxation. . . . Once more, tense those shoulder muscles again and hold the tension for a few seconds [*Pause for five seconds.*] . . . and now, very slowly and gradually, let that tension relax. . . .

Now the entire upper part of your body is feeling extremely relaxed. You can relax it even further by taking a deep breath and holding it for a few seconds. . . . And now, as you exhale, concentrate on the sensation that all the tension in your chest is flowing out, and that the muscles in your arms and hands are becoming even more relaxed. . . . Just continue breathing very slowly and naturally now as you concentrate your attention on the muscles in the abdomen.

Tense those muscles by pulling your abdomen in tightly [*Pause for five seconds*] . . . and now, very slowly and gradually, let that tension relax. Notice the pleasant difference between the feeling of tension and the feeling of relaxation. . . . Once more, tense those muscles in your abdomen, and hold the tension for a few seconds. [*Pause for five seconds.*] . . . Now, very slowly, relax those muscles again.

Now concentrate your attention on the muscles in your back. Tense those muscles by arching your back slightly. Study that feeling of tension. [*Pause for five seconds.*] Now, very slowly, let those muscles relax completely. Enjoy the pleasant contrast between the feelings of tension and the feelings of relaxation. . . . Once more, tense those back muscles and hold the tension for a few seconds. [*Pause for five seconds.*] . . . Now, very slowly and gradually, relax those muscles again. And now your entire body, all the way down to your thighs, is feeling very relaxed—calm and relaxed.

Now tense the muscles in your legs and feet by pointing your feet down, toward the floor. Study the tension you feel in your feet and in the backs of your legs. [*Pause for five seconds.*] And now, very slowly and gradually, relax that tension. Notice the pleasant contrast between the feeling of tension and the feeling of relaxation. . . . Once more, tense those muscles by pointing your feet down. Study that feeling of tension [*Pause for five seconds*] . . . and now, very slowly, relax those muscles once more. . . . This time, tense the muscles in your feet and legs by pointing your toes up, toward your head. Again feel the tension in the backs of your legs [*Pause for five seconds*] . . . and now, very slowly and gradually, relax those muscles. [*Pause for five seconds.*] Once more, tense those muscles by pointing your feet up, and hold the tension for a few seconds. . . . Once again, let that tension flow out, very slowly and gradually. Now your entire body is feeling very relaxed, calm and relaxed. You can relax even further by taking a very deep breath and holding it. . . . As you exhale, concentrate on the sensation that your body is relaxing more and more. It's so pleasant to feel so relaxed, so peaceful and relaxed. Just enjoy those very relaxing feelings.

COPY B: Insert your own Copy B here, beginning with the phrase "Now that you are so relaxed...." Before going on to Copy C, pause for sixty seconds.

COPY C: Now I am going to awaken you by counting slowly from one to ten. When I reach the count of ten, you will be completely awake, feeling alert, relaxed, and refreshed. One ... two ... three ... four ... five ... You're going to be waking up in a few minutes now ... six ... seven ... eight ... You're going to be waking up soon now ... nine ... almost awake ... ten ... Open your eyes and wake up.

It is important to get a good recording, free of distracting background sounds and spoken at a slow, even rate of speed with a pleasing tone of voice. If you are not pleased with your first effort, keep trying until you are satisfied. This may seem frustrating, but it is well worth the effort. The entire tape should run approximately twenty minutes. If it is under fifteen minutes, record it again, speaking more slowly.

For the next week or so, listen to this tape twice daily, once in the morning and once in the late afternoon or evening. A word of caution about the instructions: When you tense your muscles, don't tense them so tightly that you are straining them to the utmost, as this can give you a headache or backache. Just tense them enough so that you are very aware of the feeling of tension.

When you practice the exercise, lie down or sit in a comfortable armchair or reclining chair with your head resting against the back, your arms resting comfortably at your sides, and your legs stretched out (not crossed). If you find that you consistently fall asleep while doing the exercise, change to a slightly more upright position.

Many of my clients have used the tape to help overcome insomnia, and I have done so myself on various occasions, most recently after moving to a home where traffic noises were more noticeable than I had been accustomed to. If you have trouble falling asleep at night, you may want to play the tape again after you have gone to bed. You will probably fall asleep before it has finished playing. This is why I recommend a machine with an automatic shut-off feature. You may find that you must open your eyes when the tape tells you to wake up. If this is the case, you can record a special sleep tape that omits the wake-up instructions.

I think you will find, like most of my clients, that doing this relaxation exercise just twice a day for even one week will make you feel significantly less tense and anxious. The results you obtain will be directly related to the regularity with which you do the exercise. You will also find that you will become much more aware of muscle tension when you feel it, and you will be able to relax that tension consciously.

These relaxation instructions are modified from the progressive relaxation procedure introduced in 1939 by Edmund Jacobson, a physician. Jacobson found that pulse rate and blood pressure were diminished by deep muscle relaxation. Currently, biofeedback machines are frequently used to demonstrate changes in muscle tension and are used to train patients to relax. Although I use biofeedback occasionally, usually it is not necessary to produce change; the relaxation procedure alone, if practiced daily, will do the trick. Muscle relaxation, with or without biofeedback, has been used successfully for treating high blood pressure, tension headaches, insomnia, gastrointestinal disorders, asthma, and other stress-related disorders, as well as phobias and generalized anxiety.

One further suggestion to aid in your relaxation training: Select a signal—most often I suggest the telephone, but you may use any sound that occurs frequently—and quickly check your body for tension each time you hear that signal. If you feel tension anyplace, release it. This will help you to release the tension that builds up between relaxation practices and also make you more aware of it. Eventually, the feeling of tension will become its own signal, and you will be able to relax it automatically. At first you may have to tense the muscle, then relax it.

After practicing with Side 1 for about a week, you are ready to make the final tape for use in desensitizing yourself to the situations in which your shyness is a problem. Make this second recording on Side 2. You may want to continue to use Side 1 for general relaxation practice.

You will notice that the relaxation instructions for Side 2 are similar, but briefer, than those for Side 1. This is because you have now gained sufficient practice in relaxing your muscles so that you can quickly achieve a state of physical relaxation. To help you relax even more deeply, I am going to add some "deepening" suggestions (Copy B1).

Recording Side 2.

Record Copy A, then your own Copy B (same as Side 1), followed by Copy B1 and ending with Copy C (same as Side 1).

COPY A: Settle back very comfortably now and just let yourself relax.

Begin by concentrating on the muscles in your hands. Clench your fists tightly now and study that feeling of tension. [*Pause for five seconds.*] ... Now relax your hands ... just go on relaxing them all the way. [*Pause for five seconds.*]

Now that your hands are relaxed like that, tense the muscles in your upper arm. [*Pause for five seconds.*] ... Now relax those muscles again, and notice the difference between the feeling of tension and the feeling of relaxation. [*Pause for five seconds.*] ...

Now that your hands and arms are relaxed like that, tense the muscles in your forehead [*Pause for five seconds*] ... and now relax them. [*Pause for five seconds*] ... Now concentrate on the muscles in your eyes. Tense those by closing your eyes tightly. [*Pause for five seconds.*] ... And now relax them. [*Pause for five seconds.*] ...

Now that your forehead and eyes are relaxed like that, tense the muscles in your nose [*Pause for five seconds*] ... and now relax them. [*Pause for five seconds*] ...

Now that the upper part of your face is relaxed like that, tense the muscles in your lips [*Pause for five seconds*] ... and now relax them, let them relax completely and enjoy those pleasant feelings of relaxation. [*Pause for five seconds.*] ... Now your entire face is feeling relaxed, very pleasantly calm and relaxed.

Now tense the muscles in your chin [*Pause for five seconds*] and relax them again ... let them relax all the way. Enjoy those very pleasant relaxing feelings. [*Pause for five seconds.*] ...

Now concentrate on the muscles in your shoulders. Tense those [*Pause for five seconds*] and now relax them again. [*Pause for five seconds*] ... And now the entire upper part of your body is feeling very relaxed, calm and relaxed. You can relax even more by taking a deep breath and holding it for a few seconds ... as you exhale, concentrate on the sensation that your entire body is relaxing more and more. ...

Just continue breathing slowly and naturally now as you tense the muscles in your abdomen. [*Pause for five seconds.*] ... Now relax those muscles. [*Pause for five seconds.*] ... And now tense the muscles in your back [*Pause for five seconds*] and relax them. Your entire body, all the way down to the thighs, is feeling very relaxed now . . . calm and relaxed.

Now tense the muscles in your feet and legs by pointing your feet down [*Pause for five seconds*] . . . and now relax them again. [*Pause for five seconds.*] . . . This time, tense those muscles by pointing your feet up [*Pause for five seconds*] and now relax them. [*Pause for five seconds.*] Your entire body is feeling very relaxed now, calm and relaxed . . . very pleasantly relaxed.

You can relax even further by taking another very deep breath and holding it for a few seconds. As you exhale, concentrate on the sensation that your body is drifting deeper and deeper into a state of relaxation . . . very relaxed, very pleasantly relaxed now. . . . And now, just for a few minutes concentrate on the sound and the rhythm of your own breathing. With each breath you take you will become more and more deeply relaxed . . . as you breathe in . . . and out . . . in . . . and out . . . in . . . and out . . . in . . . and out . . . deeper and deeper . . . deeper and deeper. [*Pause for a few seconds.*] You are feeling very deeply relaxed now, very pleasantly and deeply relaxed. Completely relaxed, very calm and peacefully relaxed.

COPY B: Same as for Side 1. Again, pause for sixty seconds before continuing to Copy B1.

COPY B1. Now that you are so comfortably relaxed, visualize just as clearly as you can the situation you have selected for today. [*Pause for thirty seconds.*]

Now return to that very relaxing scene. Enjoy those peaceful feelings of calm and relaxation. [*Pause for sixty seconds.*]

Once more, visualize that other situation just as clearly as you can . . . try to see it and hear it very vividly. [*Pause for thirty seconds.*]

Now once again return to that very relaxing scene. Just put everything else out of your mind but how calm and relaxed you feel. [*Pause for sixty seconds.*]

Again, visualize that situation you are working on . . . visualize it just as clearly as you can. [*Pause for thirty seconds.*]

Now put that out of your mind and just relax again . . . visualize that very relaxing scene and enjoy those very pleasant, relaxing feelings. [*Pause for sixty seconds.*]

Once more, visualize the situation you are working on . . . try to see it very vividly. [*Pause for thirty seconds.*]

Now put that out of your mind and take yourself back to that very relaxing place . . . enjoy those very relaxing feelings. [*Pause for sixty seconds.*]

Once again, visualize that other situation very clearly . . . see it just as realistically as you can. [*Pause for thirty seconds.*]

And now put that out of your mind and return to that very relaxing place where you feel so calm, so relaxed and so peaceful. Enjoy those very calm and relaxing feelings. [*Pause for sixty seconds.*]

COPY C: Same as for Side 1.

Getting Your Act Together

You now should have a deck of index cards containing your hierarchy of anxiety-provoking scenes and a relaxing tape with two sides recorded. You should have also developed a reasonable facility for relaxation, since by this time you have been practicing twice daily for at least a week.

Now you are ready to put it all together.

Read over the script for the first (lowest-rated) item on your hierarchy. You needn't memorize it word for word, but get it clearly in mind so that you can run through it mentally. Now settle down in a comfortable place where you will not be disturbed. Take the telephone off the hook or unplug it, and put on Side 2 of your recording. Just relax now and follow instructions.

If you are like most of my clients, you will feel considerable anxiety with the first visualization of your anxiety-provoking scene, less on the second, and still less on the third. By the fifth visualization, most clients do not feel anxious; by visualizing the scene while relaxed, a process of conditioning has occurred and they are able to think about the scene without feeling anxious. Try to confine your visualization to the exact scene and script you are working on. You may want to prepare more than one script covering successive phases of the same situation. But become comfortable with the first scene before you let your thoughts carry you on ahead to the next.

People vary immeasurably, and the number of visualizations of any one scene needed for your anxiety to wear off completely may be much greater than five. If this is consistently the case for you, rerecord the last part of Side 2 to allow for as many visualizations as necessary. It is better to visualize a given scene as many times as necessary in one session for your anxiety to be eliminated. This gives you a positive feeling of accomplishment. But if you did not completely eliminate the anxiety you felt about a given scene in one session, work on that scene again the next time you practice.

While I recommend the use of a graduated hierarchy to enable you to conquer less-threatening situations first, an alternative procedure is possible. You can employ imaginary rehearsals to help you relieve anxieties about situations coming up in the immediate future whether or not you have reached that point in your hierarchy. When necessary, I use this procedure with my own clients.

A few people have trouble "getting into" a scene and need longer pauses between scenes than I have suggested. If you find this to be true for you, experiment to find the time interval you need and then record your desensitizing instructions accordingly. If you find yourself blocking out a scene, being unable to visualize it or hold onto it in your mind, that situation may be too anxiety-provoking for you to handle. Before trying it again, go back to a situation lower in your hierarchy.

I suggest one desensitizing period each day. I usually see my clients only once each week, but when you are working on your own you can make more rapid progress with daily practice.

While I initially tried to divide up my scripts equally between masculine and feminine *you* roles, my personal experience and practice have both yielded more feminine situations. So if I haven't provided the exact scripts you need, modify them or write your own.

You may not need to use my scripts at all. I'm sure that a nonshy person would be astounded at the idea that anyone would need scripts for handling such everyday situations. But I've found from experience that shy people *do not know what to say* much of the time. When I give them the words they need, they feel more confident.

However, I'm the first to admit that I'm no Neil Simon, and it's entirely possible that you can write scripts of your own that will be more helpful to you than mine.

When you're 4 On the Scene

"It's easy to do it *here*," my clients frequently say—meaning rehearse a situation in the office, either in their imagination or in a group. "But it's different doing it in real life."

Yes, it is different.

Nevertheless I find that almost invariably clients who visualize themselves in a certain scene as many times as necessary, then rehearse it alone or with others, will be able to handle that situation in real life. The first time they may experience some anxiety, but it will not be overwhelming and will decrease with repeated exposures to the situation.

To overcome social anxieties you must put yourself in test situations, and do it as frequently as possible. Obviously you cannot solve your problem if you rely on imaginary rehearsals alone. As soon as you feel reasonably secure while imagining the scene, go on out there and try it.

If you think this sounds like hard work, you're right. You must make a real effort if you are going to help yourself. Unfortunately, there is no magic solution.

Marie, who felt very nervous in groups, became quite comfortable speaking up and being the center of attention in her clinic group, but by the end of the six-week program she "hadn't found time" to attend any lectures or meetings where she could try out her skills. It was impossible to assess her progress. Betsy, on the other hand, another member of the same group, hadn't entertained people in her home for several years prior to entering the clinic but had a picnic for twenty people before the end of the program. She had clearly made excellent progress.

Suppose you have a situation coming up that is likely to be anxiety-producing. What, besides your regular desensitization sessions and rehearsals, can you do to get through it more easily?

First, if at all possible you should relax very thoroughly shortly before leaving for the date, party, interview, or whatever—and visualize yourself in the situation. Most of my clients find this extremely helpful.

Second, be prepared for conversational emergencies by having several topics which you can introduce if needed. (See Chapters 6 and 14.)

Third, consciously relax your muscles and breathe deeply immediately before and during the situation. You will find that this helps a great deal. One client who suffered from chronic colitis discovered she could usually control her stomach spasms by consciously relaxing those muscles. (This, of course, is the principle of biofeedback.)

Fourth, focus on something other than your own feelings. When you feel anxious, the tendency is to become so overly aware of what is going on internally that you shut off what is going on *externally*. In extreme cases, this may produce a feeling of dissociation, of "not really being there."

You can counteract this sensation by trying to focus your attention on something external. Many people who are phobic about traveling on trains or planes can allay or forget their anxieties by plunging into conversation with a stranger and thus getting their minds off their unpleasant sensations or the unpleasant sensations they are anticipating.

Since in social anxieties conversation is the concern, or at least part of it, focus part of your attention (the part you have been using to focus on how uncomfortable you are) on the appearance of the people you are talking to. Really look at the clothes they are wearing—the colors and textures—and be aware of the color of their eyes and hair, the way their features are put together, and any unique aspects of their appearance. Try to make a map of their faces for future reference. Don't think of what a person is thinking of you, just concentrate on what is being said and how he or she looks. Focusing on the other person this way does not mean denying your own feelings or trying to ward off an anxiety attack (this won't work); it just implies a shift of attention from inside to outside. This *will* work.

"I'll have to admit that . . ."

Fifth, consider admitting the concerns you just can't cover up. Not dwelling on the problem—just admitting it and then moving on to something else.

Some people feel that revealing feelings or admitting a deficiency is a sign of weakness. But it's possible to expend a tremendous amount of energy trying to cover up a fact that embarrasses you and may be painfully apparent anyway. It usually isn't worth covering up.

I say usually, because in certain situations you may

need to resort to evasion or subterfuge to avoid exposing something you are positive would damage you. But this happens far less often than most people think. Can you imagine yourself saying, for example, "I'll have to admit that . . ."?

"I'm shy." Is that such a terrible admission? Considering that about 40 percent of the population consider themselves somewhat shy, shyness doesn't constitute a small minority. As time goes on, I'm sure you will be feeling less and less shy. In the meantime, there's nothing wrong with admitting your shyness.

"I feel nervous." Well, what's so terrible about *that*? Feeling nervous in a new situation is a sensation you share with many others. I've heard speakers begin a speech by admitting they felt nervous—immediately capturing the sympathy of the audience.

"My blushing problem really embarrasses me." If you blush easily, you can probably learn to subdue the response in time, but until that happens, it doesn't seem reasonable to try and conceal it. I've found that many people who blush easily have a real horror of letting others see their emotions. Yet when they blush, that is exactly what happens anyway—so you might just as well verbalize your feelings.

"I don't know anyone here." That isn't disgraceful, is it? And it can be a good way of getting a conversation going. You've revealed something about yourself and made it clear that you'd like to get to know some new people.

"I need a little time to think that over." If someone asks your opinion about something you haven't made up your mind about, or asks you to go on a date or serve on a committee you're not sure about, there is nothing wrong with asking for time. When I suggested that to a group of women recently, several of them almost sighed with relief. "That sounds so simple, and so much better than trying to come up with an answer when you feel rushed and aren't sure what you want to do!" one of them exclaimed.

"I'm not familiar with this topic." Do you have to be an expert about everything? You can try to brazen your way through, but you are likely to expose your ignorance just as surely as if you'd admitted it in the first place.

"I don't know the answer." Again, you don't have to know the answer to every question. A woman told me recently that she had been offered a job that would involve giving weight-control lectures, but she refused because she didn't want to get up in front of a group. When I asked her why, she said, "Because somebody might ask me a question I wouldn't know the answer to." In general, people with a reasonably high level of self-esteem can admit they don't know the answer without feeling extremely uncomfortable.

"I made a mistake." There isn't a person alive who doesn't make a mistake once in a while, so why not admit it when you do? Trying to make up excuses or put the blame on someone else is not going to get you anywhere in the long run. A business executive told me recently that one of the major differences he observed between men and women on the job was that, if a man makes a mistake he generally says, "I goofed. I'll do it over," while a woman is more likely to come up with excuses or rationalizations. I don't know if this is true across the board, but it does represent one man's experience.

"I've forgotten your name." This one can be tricky. I've found that if I stall for a few minutes while making conversation, the elusive name will frequently spring into my mind and I can at least conclude the conversation with, "It was nice to see you, Joan"—proving that I *did* know who I was talking to. But if you feel sure this isn't going to happen, or if you are in a situation in which you must introduce people, the best thing to do is own up: "I'm terribly sorry, but I can't think of your name right now. Please help me out!"

The Power of Positive Thinking

Finally (the last-but-not-least department), develop the habit of positive thinking. Most people don't realize that thoughts can be brought under conscious control. If you repeatedly say to yourself "I'm going to feel anxious. I know I can't go through with this. What if I start blushing again?" you are going to make the situation worse and increase your chances of getting a full-blown anxiety attack.

If you say instead, "Yes, I may feel a little anxious, but it will go away soon enough and this is a situation I know I can handle. If I do feel a little anxious or blush—so what?"

I definitely recommend the "So what?" approach. It has been helpful to many people suffering not only from shyness but also from agoraphobia and other phobic disorders.

What is the very worst thing that could possibly happen? Many people who experience anxiety attacks are so busy trying to avoid them that they have never tried to figure out exactly what they are afraid of. Granted that a panic attack is a highly unpleasant experience, the anticipation of it is frequently even worse.

The "worst fear" I have most often encountered is the fear of fainting. (It is worth noting that of all the patients who have reported this fear, almost none has ever fainted.) I always ask people to imagine what would happen if they *did* actually faint. Usually they surmise realistically that someone would come rushing over to offer assistance, medical attention would be summoned, they would quickly return to consciousness—and that would be the end of the episode. They might feel embarrassed about it for a few days, but this feeling wouldn't last forever.

Sometimes, people tell me, they are in a situation, managing relatively well, when the thought "What if I get an anxiety attack?" comes to them.

The "So what?" approach is helpful here, because if you are trying to ward off an anxiety attack by tensing yourself against it, you are probably going to bring on the very thing you are hoping to avoid. It's much more therapeutic to relax and let it happen. (But try not to focus your entire thinking on the fact that it is *going* to happen!)

Let's consider some other examples of talking to yourself positively rather than negatively.

Suppose you are at a party where you don't know anyone. You are thinking of approaching a group of people. Typical negative thoughts might run like this: "Why did I come to this party anyway? Here I am again, not knowing anybody. There must be something wrong with me. If I go over and try to introduce myself to those people, I won't be able to think of anything to say. They'll all probably think I'm stupid. Probably I *am* stupid! Look at them chattering away. They certainly wouldn't want to be bothered with *me*. I don't have anything to add to the conversation, anyway."

Not much of a pep talk, is it?

But this is more or less the kind of thing shy people say to themselves. If your best friend had the kind of social insecurities you are feeling, you would undoubtedly try to think of some positive, ego-boosting things to say. You can do the same thing for yourself.

In the party situation, you might say "It looks as if I don't know anybody here. Well, that means I'll have an opportunity to meet a lot of new people. That group over there looks pretty friendly. They seem to be having a good conversation. I'm sure I can add something to it. If they're talking about something I don't know anything about, I can learn something new. I'm going to go over and introduce myself."

Let's say you are at a lecture and it is now time for the question-and-answer period. You have a question you would like to ask. A negative thinker might ruminate along these lines: "That's probably a dumb question to ask. What if somebody laughs at me? I'll bet I'm the only person in this room who doesn't already know the answer. And if I do raise my hand, my mind will go blank when I'm called on. Either that or I'll start stammering. I'd better not raise my hand."

In the same situation, positive thinking might go something like this: "This is something I need to get an answer to, and right now is my best opportunity. My question is probably just as intelligent as everyone else's. Even if it isn't, this question is important to *me*, and I have as much right to ask a question as anyone else. I'm going to write out the question so I can ask it easily without getting tongue-tied, and then I'm going to go ahead and raise my hand."

Experiments have proved that people can regulate anger, decrease interpersonal anxiety, and increase tolerance to pain by changing the way they talk to themselves. Yet most people have assumed that their thoughts were involuntary and that there was nothing they could do about them.

But you *can* do something. I have seen even severely obsessive patients gain considerable control over their thoughts by a simple procedure called the "Stop!" technique. It is so simple that at times I almost feel embarrassed when I demonstrate it to my clients. I'm sure none of them actually thinks it will work until they try it—when they discover that it works remarkably well.

How do you use the "stop" technique to get rid of negative or unwanted thoughts?

STOP!

The first step is to identify the negative thoughts you are trying to eliminate. Of course, a certain number of negatives are a part of every realistic person's way of evaluating herself or himself. But carried to extremes they can be extremely damaging.

Since you have probably felt you could do nothing about these thoughts, you may not be consciously aware of how many of them there are. So consider the question seriously now. Do you often say to yourself (and about yourself): "That was stupid," "How can you be such an idiot?", "Everybody must think I look silly," "I have nothing interesting to say," "I must be boring these people," "He couldn't possibly be interested in me," or other remarks you would readily recognize as put-downs if someone else were saying them to a third person? If you frequently think thoughts like these, you can use the "stop" technique to good advantage.

When I am demonstrating the procedure to clients, I begin by asking them to get their negative thought clearly in mind. When they indicate that they are focusing on it, in a loud voice I say "Stop!"

I wait a few seconds and then ask, "Did your thought go away?"

Almost always, the answer is yes. If it is no, I ask them to focus on the thought again and then say, even more loudly, "Stop!"

We repeat this sequence several times, with the client thinking the negative thought and me yelling "Stop!" Often they report that after the second or third time, they cannot get their thought in mind.

The next step is to have the clients think the negative thought and say "Stop!" themselves. Since I am not there with you to yell "Stop!," you will have to begin with this step. Get your thought clearly in mind and then say "Stop!" loudly. After this has been mastered, practice getting rid of the thought merely by thinking "Stop!" to yourself.

Sometimes a client reports that the thought goes away

easily enough, but soon comes back. If so, simply repeat the procedure.

If thinking "Stop!" silently is not enough, I suggest that you pinch the ball of your thumb with the fingernail of your third finger as you think "Stop!" Pick a sensitive spot. If it really hurts, so much the better. Usually this is strong enough to do the trick. If it isn't, you can wear a rubber band around your wrist and snap it as you say "Stop!" to yourself.

Before you can effectively use the "Stop!" technique or exercise other deliberate controls over your negative thoughts, you may have to train yourself to recognize them. Some of these negative thoughts are so frequent and so automatic (some psychologists label them "automatic thoughts") that you may barely be aware of them. They may occur in a kind of shorthand ("Stupid! Stupid! Stupid!") and may also occur in a parallel stream while you are thinking other thoughts or actually engaging in conversation. You may have seen this phenomenon portrayed on the screen in Woody Allen's *Annie Hall*—he was thinking one thing, saying another. As one of my clients told me in frustration, "It's like there is a little man in my head. Can't he *ever* stop talking?"

When you experience an unpleasant feeling, try to remember exactly what thoughts you were having before the feeling hit you. Sometimes your negative thoughts are in the form of visual images rather than verbalizations. If you are visualizing yourself vomiting or urinating in public, this can easily precipitate an anxiety attack. So can the thought "They're going to think I'm a fool!" These thoughts or images, or a combination, may be so much a part of you that you accept them as reality without stopping to ask yourself whether they are logical or illogical. You must work at identifying such thoughts and ridding yourself of those which are negative and irrational. You can learn to spot a negative thought when it occurs and get rid of it before it generates its usual anxiety feelings.

"You did that very well!"

At the same time you are trying to eliminate negative thoughts, you should make a strong effort to increase the positive reinforcement you are giving yourself.

When your mate, lover, friend, or child does something that pleases you, you make a point of saying so. Or at least I hope you do. Some people are quicker to criticize than to praise, but praise—positive reinforcement—has been found to be far more effective.

Even if you are generous with praise for others, you may be miserly when it comes to positive reinforcement for *yourself*. You may feel that it's egotistic to feel, and to acknowledge, that you did something well. People with this attitude are likely to be overly dependent on the opinions of others, and it's easy to see why. They have no way of validating themselves, but must have external feedback. Make a habit of verbally rewarding yourself when you feel you have done something well.

You may find that you have some negative thinking to eliminate before you are able to reward yourself effectively. What do you usually say to yourself after you've accomplished a task well?

I find that most people with low self-esteem tend to say "Well, maybe I did get a 95 on this test, but it was probably just luck. They happened to hit the few questions I knew. The next chapter in the text will probably be way too difficult for me to understand."

Or "I didn't feel too uncomfortable at this party. A few people actually talked to me. I suppose that must mean that everybody there was a nerd like me."

Or "I can't believe I asked a girl for a date and she accepted. She must be desperate. Maybe there's something wrong with her that I haven't noticed yet."

People with high self-esteem, on the other hand, are more likely to think: "A 95! Wow! I really did well on this test. If I keep this up I'll get an A in the course."

Or "I had a great time at the party. I forgot about being anxious and talked easily to a lot of people. I'm proud of the way I handled myself."

Or "It's great that an attractive girl like Suzy wants to go out with me. Things are definitely looking up. I feel good about this!"

Make a habit of reviewing your accomplishments at the end of each day and complimenting yourself for the things you did well or felt good about. Don't dwell on the negatives—accentuate the positives.

Part **3**

SCRIPTS
FOR
REHEARSAL

5
How to Introduce Yourself

Introducing yourself to a stranger or strangers is one of the tasks my shy students and clients have, almost without exception, found to be quite difficult.

Before coming to a Shyness Clinic or working on their shyness problem in individual therapy, most of them actively avoided situations where they would have to encounter this problem. If they couldn't avoid the situation, they were usually miserable and stood around on the sidelines because they didn't know anyone and didn't know how to get acquainted.

Even in situations where getting acquainted would seem very natural and the expected thing to do, it isn't easy for shy people. Many of the students in my Shyness Clinic at the Stamford branch of the University of Connecticut, where all are commuters (there are no dormitories at the branch), came to school every day for an entire semester or longer without making a single friend or even learning the name of another student.

I remember one in particular who said the Shyness Clinic was the best thing that had happened to him at the University. Prior to the clinic he had not made even one friend on campus. In the group he was pleasant and friendly, and he was an attractive and appealing young man. He was completely shocked when I suggested that he could simply introduce himself to the person sitting next to him in class.

"You mean just *cold*?" he said, his voice practically cracking. "Just walk up to somebody and tell them my name?"

I assured him that I meant just that.

"I never even thought of doing that. Are you sure it would be all right?"

I assured him that it would be.

Matt practiced in the group, introducing himself to each of the others, role-playing a situation in which they were seated next to him in class. By the following week he had introduced himself to the student next to him in his accounting class. It wasn't easy, but he did it.

Since a book can't provide you with group practice in role-playing a situation, the next best thing is to give you scripts you can use in your imaginary rehearsals. Obviously, I can't provide you with a script for every possible situation in which you might need to introduce yourself. But I've tried to describe the most typical situations presented by my clients, and in considerable detail because I've heard it said so often "If I just know ahead of time what it's going to be like, it doesn't seem so bad when I get there." Knowing what to expect—and then rehearsing it—definitely makes things easier.

Here is the basic rule to follow in inroducing yourself:

1. Do it—very directly.
2. Repeat the name of each person you meet immediately after hearing it.
3. Ask a question or make a comment about some aspect of the situation you are in, or something about the person you are speaking to—don't just stand back and wait for the other person to say something.

Most shy people have a more difficult time introducing themselves to someone of the opposite sex. For that reason, though there need be no difference in what you say, I'm including some separate scripts for both same-sex and opposite sex introductions. And, since group situations are more threatening for almost everyone than one-to-one introductions, I've included several scripts for introducing yourself to a group.

There are still some social situations, I'm told, where it isn't considered acceptable for a woman to take the initiative in introducing herself to a man. According to a recent *New York Times* article about "the mating game" at Asparagus Beach on Long Island, one attractive young woman who was observed to go up to men and introduce herself was labeled by a group of men, on the basis of this behavior, as "what used to be called a 'loose woman,'" Another twenty-four-year-old woman was quoted as saying "It's still difficult for a woman to go out and zero in on someone she likes." She reported going up to a man at the beach who was wearing a University of Wisconsin T-shirt and saying "I went to Wisconsin. Did you go there, too?" And he said "No."

Since the old rules of the game still do apply in many situations and are not likely to change overnight, a woman has to take time to evaluate the situation she is in before plunging full speed ahead. Women still have to let men take the initiative in many situations unless they are prepared to

be rejected or branded as overly aggressive. It may seem un
fair (it does). It may *be* unfair (it is). Nevertheless it is a fact.
And since this is the case, good judgment and good taste
must determine what is appropriate behavior in any given
situation.

ACT I.   ONE ON ONE

SCENE 1. Introducing yourself to another member of a
small group or seminar at first meeting

*A small room in a church, furnished with lounge chairs, which
is used for various kinds of group meetings and workshops. Tonight is the first session of a six-week program designed to help
people overcome shyness. You are desperately hoping to get
help for your problem and feel extremely uptight about attending tonight's session. While waiting for everyone to arrive,
the leader has suggested that those who are already present
break up into twos and get acquainted.*

YOU: Hi. My name is Judy Smith, What's yours?

SHE: I'm Margie Hill.

YOU: Margie, I'm glad to meet you. I don't know about you,
but I'm feeling pretty nervous about this.

SHE: Me too, Judy. Do you think this is really going to help
us?

YOU: I certainly hope it will. I've been shy all my life. How
about you?

SHE: I can't think of a time when I wasn't shy. Sometimes I
wonder how other people feel.

YOU: I know what you mean. I wonder too. But it's a relief
finding out that somebody else feels the same way.

SHE: That's for sure. I feel better now myself.

SCENE 2. Introducing yourself to a classmate, same sex.

*A college classroom. Five rows of chairs, equipped with arm-
rests, occupy the greater part of a rather dingy, medium-sized*

room with windows on one side and a blackboard on the other. The remaining two walls are painted a dull gray-green. At the front is a large wooden desk used by the professor when he is not pacing the floor or demonstrating equations. According to the round electric wall clock, the time is now exactly 6:12. Your class in business statistics is scheduled to begin at 6:15. The season is late September, soon after the beginning of the fall term.

You are a commuting student, like the majority of others at this branch of the state university where you are enrolled in an M.B.A. program.

Several students are already seated when you enter the room, but no one is talking to anyone else. There is a hushed, awkward silence, punctuated only by the sound of chairs scraping, books being deposited on chair arms, notebooks opening, ballpoints being readied.

You sit down in your usual place next to another young woman of approximately your own age.

YOU: Hi! I'm Nora Altman. What's your name?

SHE: I'm Donna Keene. Hi, Nora.

YOU: I'm glad to meet you, Donna. What do you think of this class?

SHE: Statistics isn't my thing, but so far I'm keeping up. Dr. Jones seems to make it fairly interesting. What do *you* think?

YOU: I've always liked statistics myself, and I do a lot of statistical work in my job.

SHE: What's your job?

YOU: I'm a financial analyst.

SHE: No wonder this is easy for you. I think I'm one of those people with math anxiety.

YOU: I've heard about that.

SHE: I'm hoping it will wear off.

SCENE 3. Introducing yourself to a classmate, opposite sex

Exactly the same setting as Scene 2. You enter and take a seat next to the attractive man in the second row. He is busily opening up his notebook and getting his pen ready for action *when you enter. You sit down, look at him directly, and speak in a clear, firm tone.*

YOU: I'm Nora Altman. What's your name?

HE: I'm Don Keene. Hi, Nora.

YOU: I'm glad to meet you, Don. I don't know anyone here, do you?

HE: No, I don't—or should I say didn't? Now I know you. Are you in the degree program, Nora?

YOU: Yes, only two more years to go at my present rate of speed. How about you?

HE: I think we'll be finishing about the same time if we both hang in there.

YOU: I'm planning to hang in, aren't you?

HE: Yes, in my business you need an M.B.A. to get ahead.

YOU: What's your business?

HE: I'm in banking. What do you do?

YOU: I'm a financial analyst.

SCENE 4. Introducing yourself to one other person, same sex, in·a business situation

A hotel meeting room, set up for a two-day seminar on Business Communication, being attended by representatives of various companies in the utility field. Across the front of the room is a long table covered with company brochures, government publications, and other handouts. At the center of the table is a microphone, with an array of wires leading in different directions. Halfway down the middle aisle a slide carousel is being set up by a young, casually dressed woman. Seats for approximately forty people have been arranged in rows of five behind folding tables.

You enter and take a seat at one of the tables near the front, next to a man in a gray flannel suit.

YOU: Hello. I'm Joe Ridgely from UT&T. I don't think we've met.

HE: Joe, it's good to meet you. I'm Win Rogers from Amalgamated. Do you come to many of these seminars?

YOU: I've only joined the company recently. Do you find them helpful?

HE: On the whole, yes. I always come away with some new ideas.

YOU: Communications is such an important field that I feel like I'm bound to learn something here I can put into practice.

HE: They have an impressive list of speakers, too. I'm anxious to hear what Tom Wilson has to say.

YOU: Oh, yes—the *Times* columnist. I agree with you. That should be interesting.

HE: How about some coffee, Joe? I think we have time before the meeting starts.

YOU: Good idea.

SCENE 5. Introducing yourself to another person, opposite sex, in a business situation

Exactly the same setting as Scene 4. You enter and take a seat next to an attractive young woman in a softly tailored blue suit. Without hesitating, you turn and speak to her directly.

YOU: Hello. I'm Joe Ridgely from UT&T. I don't think we've met.

SHE: Hello, Joe, I'm glad to meet you. I'm Wendy Rogers from Amalgamated.

YOU: Are you new there or have I just missed you before? I'm in your office quite frequently.

SHE: You're very observant. I *am* new—just started last month, in fact.

YOU: Do you like it?

SHE: I'll have to let you know later; I'm not sure yet. I'm one of the only women there who isn't a secretary. I guess I feel like a pioneer.

YOU: I like pioneers.

SCENE 6. Introducing yourself to another person, same sex, in a social situation

A living room in a split-level house. The room is tastefully dec-orated in hues of gold and brown. The furniture is primarily modern but a few interesting antique pieces, together with the woodcuts and paintings on the wall, reveal the owner to be a person of considerable taste and probably considerable money as well. A large coffeemaker has been set up on a low table in the center of the room.

The occasion for the gathering is the formation of a new amateur theater group, announced in last week's newspaper. Volunteers from the community interested in participating in the new enterprise as actors, technicians, stagehands, ticket-sellers, and so on, were invited to attend.

Although you feel rather apprehensive about the prospect of conversation in an unfamiliar situation, you park your car, take a few deep breaths and walk up to the door, where you are greeted by a friendly looking man.

HE: Hi! I'm Josh Edwards.

YOU: I'm Joni Smith.

HE: Come in and meet everybody, Joni. We're getting started in just a few minutes, so why don't you help yourself to a cup of coffee?

YOU: Thanks, I will.

You enter the room and walk over to the coffeemaker, where most of the group is congregated. You approach another woman about your own age.

YOU: Hi! I'm Joni Smith. Have I missed anything? I'm a lit-tle late.

SHE: Hi, Joni. I'm Frankie Peale. Nothing has really hap-pened yet. Are you going to try out for a role in the first play?

YOU: No, my acting experience is limited to a walk-on in jun-ior high school. I'd be too nervous. Do you act?

SHE: I've been in a few amateur theatricals and am hoping to get started again. I just moved to Wilton a few months ago, so this seemed like an ideal group to join.

YOU: Where did you move here from?

SHE: I've been living in Dallas for the past few years, but I grew up in this area. It's nice to be back.

SCENE 7. Introducing yourself to another person, opposite sex, in a social situation

Exactly the same setting as Scene 6. You enter, walk over to the group by the coffee machine, and approach a man of approximately your own age.

YOU: Hello. I'm Joni Smith. Have I missed anything? I think I'm a little late.

HE: Hello, Joni. I'm Frank Peale. No, you haven't missed anything. Things haven't really gotten rolling yet. People are just exchanging ideas about what we're doing here. I'm interested in designing scenery. How about you?

YOU: Actually, I'm not sure. I've just always enjoyed the theater and thought it would be fun to get involved, so I'm willing to do anything that needs doing.

HE: Maybe you'd like to work on the scenery committee.

YOU: I think I would like to.

HE: Good, it's a deal.

SCENE 8. Introducing yourself to another person, same sex, at a singles party

A singles party. A large YMCA meeting room, sparsely furnished, has been set up for a wine-and-cheese-tasting event. Platters of cheese and jugs of wine occupy most of a long table, decorated with a printed paper tablecloth, at one end of the room. The wooden floor is bare. A few straight chairs are lined up along one wall.

At a smaller table near the door, a rather attractive woman of about thirty is collecting the three-dollar admission fee from each new arrival. A stack of blank nametags and a felt marking pen are on the table near the money box.

This is your first singles party and you look around uncertainly, feeling a twinge of apprehension as you enter. You quietly tell yourself to relax, at the same time consciously re-

*leasing the tension in your neck and shoulders. You hand your
three dollars to the woman behind the money box, who smiles
pleasantly and directs you to the nametags. After attaching
your badge for the evening, you cast your eyes around the
room, and spot a lone individual standing silently by the
cheese display. You approach.*

YOU: Hello. My name is Dale O'Neal. What's yours?

HE: Hi, Dale, I'm Peter Richmond. Have you been to any of these parties before?

YOU: No. I've read their notices in the paper, but this is the first time I've managed to get here. How about you?

HE: I came once before, but there don't seem to be any of the same people here.

YOU: Maybe they all met somebody and didn't have to come back. I was divorced recently and am trying to get back into circulation.

HE: Well, this is the way to do it—so they tell me.

SCENE 9. Introducing yourself to another person, opposite sex, at a singles party

*Exactly the same setting as Scene 8. You approach a lone indi-
vidual of the opposite sex.*

YOU: Hi. My name is Dale O'Neal. What's yours?

SHE: I'm Petra Richmond. Nice to meet you, Dale. Are you new to the group? I haven't seen you here before.

YOU: Yes, I was divorced a few months ago. This is my first singles party. How about you?

SHE: I've been divorced a little over a year. I think you'll find that this group has a lot to offer—there are discussion groups, tennis parties, dances—different things. And there are always a lot of new faces.

YOU: I know I need to make new friends. But it wasn't easy to make myself come tonight. It's like being a teenager all over again.

SHE: I know exactly what you mean. But it does get easier. I think everyone feels just like you do when they have to start socializing again.

YOU: It's encouraging to know I'm not the only one.

ACT II. PARTY LINE

SCENE 1. Introducing yourself in a small group, where this is part of the routine first-night procedure

The faculty lounge of a small university where a group therapy program is being conducted. As is customary in most such groups, each member has been asked to "Introduce yourself, tell us a little about yourself, and explain briefly why you are here."

You consciously try to relax and remind yourself that everyone else is probably feeling nervous too. You figure out what you are going to say so you will not be unprepared when your turn comes.

YOU: I'm Margaret Penfield. I live in Riverside and am working on my master's degree in business administration. I work part time for an accounting firm in Stamford. My shyness is causing me a lot of problems at school and at work. I'm always afraid I will be called on in class and do anything I can to avoid having that happen. I never speak up voluntarily in a group. I haven't made any friends at school, even though the same people are in most of my classes. I always stand back and hope that someone else will make the first move. On the job, I can handle the accounting work easily, but dealing with my boss, the office staff, and the clients gets me so nervous that sometimes I think I should do something else. The trouble is that I can't think of any other field where this would be any less of a handicap.

SCENE 2. Introducing yourself to two or more people, same sex, in a social situation

A cocktail party to which you were invited because the hostess is a friend of your mother's. She greeted you graciously when you arrived, but you soon find yourself on your own.

You approach the bar, set up in the elegant dining room, and ask for a glass of white wine. You walk slowly back into the living room, where people are chatting in an animated fashion, and look around for another guest who appears to be alone. But everyone seems to be talking to somebody else. You hesitate, getting your courage up to introduce yourself to a group of people. You walk over to three people who are laughing and talking as you arrive. They pause briefly and you take advantage of the momentary lull to introduce yourself.

YOU: Hello. I'm Clare Bradley. I don't seem to know anyone here. May I join you?

THEY: Nice to meet you, Clare. I'm Joanna Richardson. I'm Della Rivers.
I'm Sandy McFarlane. We were talking about the plans for the new community art center. Did you know they're taking over the old library building?

YOU: Yes, I did hear that. It seems like the perfect place for an art gallery—right there on the river.

DELLA: I think the artists in the area will enjoy having such an attractive place to exhibit.

YOU: Are you an artist?

DELLA: Yes—and no. I'm in advertising, and I'm a Sunday painter.

YOU: What kind of painting do you do?

DELLA: Watercolors, landscapes mostly, but I'm trying to branch out and be a little more adventurous.

YOU: I think I've seen some of your work. Did you have some paintings on display at the State National Bank last month?

DELLA: Yes. You're good to remember!

SCENE 3. Introducing yourself to two or more people, mixed group, in a social situation

Exactly the same setting as Scene 2, but this time you approach one other woman and two men who are talking together.

YOU: Hello. I'm Clare Bradley. I don't seem to know anyone here. May I join you?

THEY: It's nice to meet you, Clare. I'm Jon Richardson.
I'm Dick Rivers.
I'm Sandy McFarlane. We were talking about the plans for the new community art center. Did you know they're taking over the old library building?

YOU: Yes, I did hear that. It seems like the perfect place for an art gallery—right there on the river.

DICK: I think the artists in the area will enjoy having such an attractive place to exhibit.

YOU: Are you an artist?

DICK: Yes—and no. I'm in advertising. I'm a Sunday painter too.

YOU: What kind of painting do you do?

DICK: Watercolors, landscapes mostly, but I'm trying to branch out and be a little more adventurous.

YOU: I think I've seen some of your work. Did you have some paintings on display at the State National Bank last month?

DICK: Yes. You're good to remember.

SCENE 4. Introducing yourself to two or more people at a singles party

A tennis party at an indoor tennis club, one of a series of Sunday-evening "mixed scrambles" for singles. Through the glass windows on each side of the comfortable lounge furnished with low-slung couches, easy chairs, and soft drink machines, white-clad players can be seen warming up. All six courts are in use. At the desk, a young woman in a tennis outfit is checking off reservations, taking names, and giving instructions to each new arrival, who draws a number out of a box—on red paper for the women, blue for the men.

A large chart with players' numbers, court numbers, and times is prominently on display beside the desk. A large sign above it reads: "Play a total of eight games and report your score to the desk after each match. When the horn blows, find your partner and start to play."

You have just drawn your number and determined by a look at the chart that your starting point is Court Six with number 24 as your partner. It is now 6:45, and play is to begin at 7:00. You walk over to two men standing near the center of the room. You feel somewhat nervous, but you know from prior experience that if you start talking to someone, you will feel better.

YOU: Hi. I'm Ginger Nevins—Number Twenty-three. Is Number Twenty-four here, by any chance?

THEY: No, sorry, I'm Fifteen—Jack Robson.
I'm Nine—Tim Wilson.

YOU: Have you been to one of these things before? I haven't, and I don't mind admitting I feel a little nervous.

YOU: I came once last month, and it was a lot of fun.

TIM: I play here once a week in a foursome, but this is my first time at one of these parties.

YOU: Jack, what was the level of play?

JACK: A mixed bag. Do you play a lot?

YOU: Yes, but I'm afraid it won't show. When I'm nervous I don't play well.

JACK: Don't worry, you'll get warmed up after a few minutes. And most people are here as much for the party as for the tennis.

SCENE 5. Introducing yourself to two or more people in a vacation setting

A hotel dining room, moderately luxurious, overlooking the beach in Jamaica. The waiters are attired in black trousers and bright blue jackets. The guests are wearing a variety of outfits, ranging from long evening dresses and high-heeled silver pumps to open-neck sport shirts and Bermuda shorts. Bouquets of red hibiscus adorn each table. Sliding glass windows at the end of the room open onto a flagstone terrace set up for al fresco dining and dancing. The night is warm and balmy.

It is the first evening after your arrival by jet from New York, along with some two hundred other participants in the package tour you chose for your winter vacation. A majority of the travelers appear to be married couples, or at least couples traveling together, but there are a number of other singles like yourself. One large section of the hotel's dining room has been assigned to the tour group, and guests are seated at tables of four and six on a first-come, first-served basis.

As you enter the room the smiling maitre d' comes forward and ushers you to a table already occupied by two men dressed in sports clothes and a woman in a long flowered skirt and low-necked blouse.

YOU: Hello! I'm Nancy Jones.

THEY: Hi, Nancy. I'm Bob Newcomb, and this is my wife Joy. I'm Jim Green, Nancy.

YOU: Good to meet you all. Let's see—Bob, Joy, and Nancy. I think I have it.

JOY: What do you think of Galloping Bay so far?

YOU: It's a sensational spot! The view from my room is breathtaking. It's just what I was hoping for. What's your reaction?

JIM: After the cold weather up north, this looks like the perfect getaway. I'm hoping to soak up a lot of sun and do some snorkeling.

YOU: Oh, I was thinking of that too. But I didn't bring any equipment. Did you?

JIM: I brought my own stuff, but I know they rent it here too.

JOY. I tried snorkeling once, but it wasn't my thing. I felt like suffocation was just around the corner.

JIM: It does feel strange at first, but you get over it. I'm thinking of taking some scuba lessons this winter. That would really get to you, Joy!

JOY: Don't even mention it. I read an article in the *Times* about somebody doing scuba diving in Long Island Sound—using a flashlight to see the fish on the bottom. No, thanks.

YOU: I agree with you, Joy. That doesn't sound a bit tempting.

Act III. The Face Is Familiar But . . .

Scene 1. Reintroducing yourself in a casual situation to someone you've met briefly before

The produce section of a supermarket. It is noon on a Wednesday and the store is relatively uncrowded. You are squeezing avocados to select a ripe one when you look up and detect a familiar face across the aisle from you, judiciously examining heads of lettuce. A pair of brown eyes meets yours briefly, passing on with no indication of recognition.

Your first instinct is to turn your attention back to the avocados or hastily flee to another aisle, but you decide to make the extra effort you have promised yourself to exert in such situations from now on. You walk over to the lettuce display.

YOU: Hello there. I'm Ellie Duncan. We met at jogging practice last week at the Y.

SHE: Oh, Ellie! I didn't recognize you out of your jogging suit. I'm Fran Wharton.

YOU: How's the jogging going?

SHE: Dogged determination keeps me in there running. If everyone else in the world can do it, so can I.

YOU: Did you happen to hear Jim Fixx speak last week in Greenwich?

SHE: No, I thought of it, but I didn't quite get there. Did you go?

YOU: Yes, and it was interesting. You'd have enjoyed it.

Scene 2. Reintroducing yourself in a social situation to someone you've met briefly before

A dinner meeting of a professional society to which you belong. A private dining room in a Holiday Inn has been arranged for tables of eight. The first course, fruit cocktail, is already in place.

Following a cash-bar cocktail hour in an adjoining room, the lights dim twice in rapid succession to indicate that it is time to move on to dinner. You follow the crowd as it moves into the dining room, and approach a table where several people are already seated.

YOU: Is this place taken, or may I join you?

HE: No, it isn't taken—please sit down.

YOU: Thanks. I'm Marge Palmer, Dan. We met last summer at the dinner meeting in Hartford—B. F. Skinner was the speaker.

HE: Of course, I remember now. How have you been, Marge? Are you still with the clinic in White Plains?

YOU: No, I'm in private practice now, and do some group work at the university counseling center. How about you? Are you still teaching?

HE: Yes, still at Southern.

SCENE 3. Reintroducing yourself to someone from the distant past

The opening reception for a college reunion. A brightly striped canvas tent has been erected on the college green, and members of the class of '69 are dressed uniformly in striped red-and-white cotton slacks and red T-shirts with the college name prominently emblazoned on the front. The women have identical T shirts and red-and-white striped wraparound skirts. All are wearing large round nametags, white with red lettering.

You find yourself standing next to a man you haven't seen once since graduation, but recall clearly from the sociology class where you sat next to each other. But he is looking at you blankly, making you wonder if you have aged drastically or just didn't make much of an impression in the first place. You put these thoughts out of your mind.

YOU: Greg, I'm Ed Allen. We sat next to each other in sociology.

HE: Ed! It's great to see you. Can you believe it's been ten years?

YOU: So far, everybody looks pretty much the same. What have you been doing since I saw you last?

HE: A few years at law school, then joined a firm in New York, and moved out to Dallas two years ago. I'm turning into a Texan. What are you doing these days?

YOU: I'm in the advertising business—a partner in a small firm in New York. I get to Dallas once in a while.

HE: Give me a call next time you're in town.

YOU: Thanks, I'll try to.

SCENE 4. Reintroducing yourself to someone who obviously doesn't remember you

A cocktail party. Your hostess is introducing you to a woman you have met before, a professor at the local university. You remember the meeting clearly but it is apparent that she does not.

HOSTESS: Janet, I want you to meet Katie Adams.

JANET: Hello, Katie, it's nice to meet you.

YOU: It's nice to see you again, Dr. Jones. We met once before, at an economics department party.

DR. JONES: Let's see, that must have been in January.

YOU: That's right. I remember that we were talking about the university's plans for expansion.

DR. JONES: I think I do remember now, Katie. It's nice to meet you again.

SCENE 5. Reintroducing yourself to someone whose name you've forgotten

A supermarket aisle. You find yourself staring at the woman next to you and feel certain you have met, but you can't remember her name.

YOU: Hello. I'm Barbara Elliot. Haven't we met?

SHE: Oh, yes. I'm Joy Aldrich. I knew you looked familiar.

YOU: We were in an exercise class together at the Y, I think. It's coming back to me.

SHE: Yes, of course. That seems like a long time ago. Are you doing anything along those lines now?

YOU: No, I've switched to jogging. How about you?

Act IV. Isn't It Time We Got Acquainted?

Scene 1. Exchanging names with someone you've conversed with informally on several occasions

An adult education painting class, meeting in a large high school classroom. A demonstration easel is set up in front of the room facing the class, with paints and palette on a table nearby. Slightly to the left, a still life composed of a basket, a wine bottle, and several fresh fruits has been carefully arranged.

You enter with your painting gear and take the same seat you have occupied since the course began several weeks ago. Next to you is the same attractive young man who has been in that seat each week.

Each week you've wanted to introduce yourself, but something has stopped you. This time you are more determined. You smile at him pleasantly and he smiles back, saying nothing.

YOU: Isn't it time we got acquainted? I'm Donna Devon.

HE: I'm Scott Everett. Hi, Donna. I've been admiring your painting style.

YOU: Thanks, Scott. I like your work too. Have you been painting long?

HE: For a few years, off and on. Not very consistently, though.

YOU: I know what you mean. I keep getting sidetracked too. And then I find I have to enroll in another class to get myself going again.

Scene 2. Exchanging names with someone you've just had a brief, pleasant conversation with

The interior of a commuting train on the New Haven division. The conductor has just announced that the next station stop is Stamford—your destination. The train begins to slow down and passengers are standing up in the aisle with brief cases and shopping bags. You are still seated next to a very attractive young woman with whom you have been chatting animatedly since 125th Street.

YOU: This is the first time I've actually been sorry it was time to get off the train! It's been fun talking to you. By the way, my name is Alex O'Donohue. What's yours?

SHE: Edwina Finch.

YOU: You live in Darien, don't you? Are you in the phone book?

SHE: Yes, and yes.

YOU: I'll call you. Goodbye for now.

SHE: Bye, Alex.

How to Get 6 a Conversation Going

Getting a conversation going follows logically after introducing yourself. You don't want to exchange names and then just stand there. For some shy people, the introduction itself is the biggest stumbling block—once they've accomplished that much, things tend to go smoothly. For others the introduction is only a prelude to even greater difficulties in the form of *"Now* what do I say?"

Of course, there are some situations where it's more logical to begin a conversation first and introduce yourself later—or not at all. If you start talking to someone standing in line next to you, someone in a singles bar, or someone seated next to you on a train or plane, you're probably not going to introduce yourself initially. But you might do so at the end of the conversation if you've enjoyed it and hope to see the person again. And you never know what may develop: Edward Durrell Stone, the famous architect, met a fashion writer on a transatlantic flight and proposed to her before the plane landed.

Your initial remark or question to a person you don't know most often concerns some aspect of the situation you are in, or some observation about the person you're talking with. This could relate to appearance, an item of clothing you admire, or something the person is carrying which offers a conversational jumping-off point.

It's natural to say to a man with a large Willoughby-Peerless paper bag, "It looks like you've just bought a new camera," or to ask someone with a *New York Times* open to a half-finished crossword puzzle, "How did you get along with the upper right-hand corner?" (I attended a crossword puzzle contest a few months ago, and discovered that crossword puzzle fans can talk endlessly about the solution to 6 Across or 7 Down, and how they thought of it or didn't.)

I also think that in many situations it is perfectly acceptable to say to someone "You look like someone I'd like to know. My name is Rob Elliott. What's yours?" Some people might think this would be coming on too strong, and I doubt if most women would be comfortable saying that to a man or that most men would respond favorably. But a man who is reasonably sure of himself could definitely get away with it, and most women would be pleased with such an approach.

Some people experience their greatest discomfort in talking to strangers, while others take strangers in stride but feel tongue-tied talking to casual acquaintances, people they are dating, in-laws, or other relatives. In beginning a conversation with someone you already know, it is comfortable to ask about what they have been doing since you last met, to refer to your last meeting, or to ask the person's opinion about some topic of common interest. Conversation is a lot like everything else in life from one point of view, at least: the more you put into it, the more you get out.

There are two very basic rules for keeping a conversation going:

1. Try never to ask a question that can be answered "Yes" or "No." Don't ask "Did you like Mexico?" but "What did you like best about Mexico?" (and follow that up with "That's interesting . . . why?").

2. Try never to *answer* a question with a mere "Yes" or "No," even if the other person has asked it in such a way that this is a possible response. Always give more than the barest minimum reply. If you're asked "What have you been doing since I saw you last?" don't say "Working" and leave it at that. Be more explicit and expansive: "Going to school in Los Angeles, clerking in a department store in San Francisco, and tutoring here in Stamford." This kind of reply provides several possible directions for further discussion, such as "What was the West Coast like?" or "How did you like waiting on customers compared to tutoring children?"

You'll discover, like Anita, a member of one of my Shyness Clinics, that if you put in more of yourself the other person will usually meet you halfway. Anita reported a conversation with a co-worker after a business meeting she had attended in another city. "He always asks me how the meeting goes, and in the past I always said 'Fine.' This time I told him what happened at the meeting. And it really worked out well. We had a very interesting conversation."

"Now when I'm in a situation where I might talk to somebody, I picture myself saying just a word or two the way I used to," Anita continued. "Then I picture myself saying more—and then I just make myself go ahead and say more. It's made a big difference."

Sandy, another member of the same clinic, reported a

weekend conversation with a young girl at a graduation party she had attended. "She was really hard to talk to," Sandy said. "No matter what I asked her, she just kept replying in monosyllables. I realized that was how I used to sound. No wonder people thought I was hard to talk to. I was!"

As a former newspaper feature writer, I have occasionally had the experience of interviewing people who had done or were doing something interesting but were simply not able to talk about it in an interesting way. They responded to questions with one- or two-word answers: "Yes," "No," "Fine," "So-so," "Not bad," "Very interesting," etc. And there is no way, short of outright fabrication, to make an interesting feature article out of material like that.

There's no way to make an interesting conversation out of it either. So make a special effort to avoid monosyllables. You'll find that your efforts in this direction will pay off quickly.

Make a habit of conversing with as many people as you can, especially now, when you are trying so hard to overcome shyness. Practice may not make your conversation perfect, but I guarantee that it will drastically improve your performance.

Many of my shy clients have found it useful to keep a running scorecard for conversation. The objective of this exercise is to speak to as many people as possible, people you don't ordinarily speak to. (A conversation with your mother doesn't count, unless you are in the habit of not speaking to your mother!) I ask people to record each potential conversational encounter and to give themselves a score of 0 for each encounter where they say nothing, a score of 1 if they say "Hello," 2 if they say "Hello" and make at least one additional remark, and 3 if they have a conversation lasting three minutes or longer. Shoot for as many threes as possible.

When you approach conversational practice with a determined attitude, you'll find that you have been passing up many opportunities every day. You can converse with the person next to you at the meat counter, the woman behind you at the cleaners, the clerk in the hardware store, the person next to you in class, the waitress at the restaurant where you have lunch every day, and the man who delivers a package to your house—to mention only a few possibilities. I'm always suspicious when people tell me "It was a quiet week—I didn't see anyone to talk to," because usually that just isn't so.

Some people dismiss "small talk," and these exercises to improve small talk, as a useless waste of time. It really isn't. Small talk gives you and a new acquaintance an opportunity to determine whether you would be interested in exploring a closer relationship. Herbert Fensterheim, a well-known behavior therapist, schematizes conversational content as a series of concentric circles, the E or outermost level representing "small talk." ("My name is Jane Jones. . . . I like chocolate ice cream. . . . Did you hear the score in the Yankees game today?") The A or inner circle represents the most personal disclosures, which would only be made in an intimate relationship. Obviously there are many levels in between these two extremes.

This chapter will be mostly concerned with small talk.

I recommend to shy clients that they develop a comfortable repertoire of small talk, a kind of memory bank they can draw on when necessary. Especially before going on a date you feel nervous about, it's a good idea to think of possible conversational topics ahead of time. These might include current good movies you have seen (try to pull together some thoughts about each movie and your personal reactions to it); good books you have read lately or are reading; topics in the news that interest you; interesting experiences you have had recently.

Shy people frequently tell me they don't have any interesting experiences ("Nothing ever happens to me"), but this isn't so. It's all in the way you look at what happens. One of my first serious boyfriends had such a talent for observing and relating his experiences that he could make a fascinating adventure out of a trip to the laundromat. And one of my favorite clients, a girl in her twenties who is not only painfully shy but has other serious problems, possesses such a comic gift that she can make me laugh until I cry while she recounts what to someone else would be a week in which "nothing happened." (There is more on this subject in Chapter 14.)

Introducing Others

Many shy people feel particularly inept when it comes to introducing two people who are strangers to each other. Etiquette provides clear standards for who to present to whom, but the question of what to say next is not as easily answered. Several members of my Shyness Clinics have been women planning weddings for their daughters and dreading, most of all, mingling with guests at the reception and trying to introduce everybody to everybody else. Another woman, who also shied away from introductions and felt very uncertain of herself in the role of hostess, had a picnic for twenty people before the end of the five-week program. "Everything went fine and I didn't have trouble with any introductions but one," she reported. "I forgot my son's name!"

Almost everyone has experienced the sudden sinking feeling that comes when you turn smilingly to introduce someone and realize at the same instant that your mind has gone totally blank. About all you can do is admit your predicament and apologize. The condition is, of course, temporary—and the cause is usually anxiety.

Assuming that the situation isn't quite so drastic, the best way to get two people talking is to provide some information along with the introductions. Occupational clues are always good, provided the person has an interesting occupation (and provided the other person doesn't happen to be embarrassingly unemployed): "This is Janet Bendell, who has her own advertising agency; this is Bill Dyer, editor of the *News.*"

One friend of mine has a particular aversion to occupational introductions and conversations, though she herself has a career that invariably sounds fascinating to others and puts her constantly in touch with interesting people (she is a researcher for *People* magazine). Many other kinds of information can be used to get a conversation going. For example: "This is Rich Stoddard, who's just back from Acapulco; This is Carmen Ramos, who comes from Peru; This is Scott Ogilvie, one of the best tennis players in town; This is Katie Wilkins, who won first place in the art show last week."

Unless *both* people you've introduced are excruciatingly shy, they will be able to start talking easily once you've given them something to go on.

A word of caution about titles: If you use them, be sure you are correct. A Miss doesn't like to be called a Mrs., and a doctor will usually not appreciate being introduced as Mister. If you are not sure which form of address a person prefers, ask. I am very familiar with this problem, since I am constantly being addressed and introduced as Mrs. Powell—which I am not and have never been.

ACT I. IS THERE A STRANGER IN THE HOUSE?

SCENE 1. Starting a conversation with someone next to you in a supermarket line

The checkout counter of a busy supermarket. The teenage cashier is doing a slow job of packing. You are third in line, but it looks like a long wait. The woman ahead of you has a shopping cart overflowing with groceries. You decide to take advantage of the opportunity to practice your conversational skills. You remind yourself that you don't have to say something brilliant; you just have to say something.

YOU: That's quite an unpacking chore you're going to have.

SHE: Yes, unloading is the worst part. In fact, I'm already dreading it.

YOU: This heat doesn't help much either.

SHE: The heat doesn't bother me much. Compared to where I used to live, this is almost cool.

YOU: You must be from the Southwest.

SHE: Yes, I moved here recently from Phoenix.

SCENE 2. Starting a conversation with a stranger on a train or plane

An airplane. Dinner has been served and the stewardesses are busily going up and down the aisle collecting empty trays and pouring more coffee. You are enjoying your second cup of coffee when you notice that the man next to you has already taken his briefcase out again and seems to be getting back to work.

YOU: You don't give yourself much time off, do you?

HE: I'm on my way to a job interview, and I'm trying to bone up on a few facts I'm going to need. I guess I'm nervous about it. It's a job I'd really like to have.

YOU: No wonder you're studying then. How would you feel about moving to New York?

HE: Oh, the job wouldn't be in New York. It would be in Chicago. The company headquarters is in New York so I'm being interviewed there. Right now I'm working for the same company in St. Louis. If I get the position in Chicago I'll be the regional sales manager.

YOU: Good luck with your interview. I guess you'd like to get back to your studying now.

SCENE 3. Starting a conversation with someone of the opposite sex whom you see repeatedly in the same situation

A town beach in a small community on Cape Cod where you have gone for a two-week vacation. The white sand is spotted with brightly colored beach umbrellas, mothers with children building sand castles, and people of all ages soaking up the warm August sun.

You peel off your Amherst College T shirt and settle down with your portable radio near your favorite dune. Just as you are about to roll over on your stomach, you notice with pleasure that the same attractive blonde who has occupied the towel near yours for the past three days has just arrived again. She is wearing a sweatshirt labeled SMITH. You feel annoyed with yourself for not having had the nerve to initiate a conversation yesterday or the day before, but are delighted to have another opportunity. This time you make up your mind to say something before your courage deserts you.

YOU: Hi there! I was hoping you'd come again today.

SHE: Oh, hi, yourself. Yes, I have another week. I get the impression you go to Amherst.

YOU: Yes, I'm a senior there. You must go to Smith.

SHE: Yes, how did you guess? Nothing like wearing an advertisement, is there?

YOU: I'm glad you did. It helped me get up the nerve to speak to you. I'm Joe Miller.

SHE: I'm Kathy Johnson.

ACT II. GETTING TO KNOW YOU

SCENE 1. Starting a conversation with someone at the second meeting of a small group program

The faculty lounge of a small university where the second session of a group therapy program in overcoming shyness is about to begin. You have arrived a few minutes ahead of time. You sit down next to another member of the group. Although your natural inclination is to sit there and say nothing, you re-

mind yourself that you are here for conversational practice. You are frantically trying to remember her name, but are unsuccessful. (Of course, if you do remember, you simply begin by saying, "Hi, Margie.")

YOU: Hi! It's nice to see you again. But I've forgotten your name. Mine's Judy Smith.

SHE: I'm Margie Hill. How have you been, Judy?

YOU: Pretty good. I've been trying harder. I still feel pretty shy, but maybe not as bad as last week. I've talked to quite a few strangers.

SHE: Me too. The first couple of times were really hard. But it seems to be getting easier.

YOU: I feel more comfortable here this week, too. How about you?

SHE: I feel the same way.

SCENE 2. Starting a conversation with someone you see frequently but don't know well.

A high school classroom where an adult education class in conversational Spanish is being conducted. It is a few minutes before the class is to begin, and the instructor is busy writing a list of vocabulary words on the blackboard.

As usual, you sit down next to a tall man who wears glasses and seldom says much in class. When he does speak, his Spanish accent is easy and natural-sounding.

YOU: Hi, Bob. Have you been speaking much Spanish since last week?

HE: No, not much. How about you?

YOU: I don't have anyone to talk to between classes here. I'm practicing up for a trip to Mexico next summer. You go to Latin America often, don't you?

HE: Yes, my company has offices in Argentina and Peru.

YOU: Is that how you acquired such an authentic accent?

HE: No, I grew up in Argentina speaking both Spanish and English. But we came back to the states when I was twelve, and I didn't speak Spanish for quite a few years—until I started my present job.

YOU: I'd like to travel more often myself. But I suppose when you have to, it stops being so much fun.

SCENE 3. Starting a conversation with someone at work

A modern, attractively furnished office in the suburban corporate headquarters of a manufacturing firm. It is a Monday morning just before nine. Most of the office personnel—secretaries, typists, receptionist—are at their desks. The executives and middle-management personnel are beginning to drift in.

You have recently joined the firm as a financial analyst. The office next to yours is occupied by a young woman who holds a position similar to yours. You have had a few brief business-oriented conversations with her and would like to establish a friendlier relationship.

You have just entered your office when you hear Marjorie approaching hers. You walk to the door and greet her as she comes in.

YOU: Good morning, Marjorie. Have a nice weekend?
SHE: Yes, I managed to keep pretty busy, and that's what I like.
YOU: It looks like you got some sun.
SHE: I certainly did! Almost too much, but not quite. I was on the tennis court for three hours yesterday and it was hot!
YOU: You must be a good tennis player.
SHE: I'm a B Club player. Do you play?
YOU: Yes, I try to get out at least twice a week. Maybe we could play sometime.
SHE: That sounds like a good idea.

ACT III. YOU'RE AMONG FRIENDS

SCENE 1. Thinking of something to say when the conversation goes dead

You are having lunch with a friend, someone you know relatively well. You had been discussing the wedding of a mutual friend, but suddenly that topic of conversation has exhausted itself. You find yourselves sitting there staring at each other. Your mind goes blank for a minute. Calmly you tell yourself to relax. You flip quickly through your repertoire of conversational topics and come up with something appropriate to the situation.

YOU: Have you seen *Heaven Can Wait?*

SHE: No, have you?

YOU: I went the other night, and it's terrific. I don't know when I have laughed so much. Warren Beatty is really talented—he produced it, directed it, and starred in it. And he's so attractive too. You shouldn't miss it.

SHE: I won't. I enjoy a movie that makes me laugh. I saw *Foul Play* the other evening, with Goldie Hawn and Chevvy Chase—it was very entertaining too. If you haven't seen it, I recommend it. They called it a comedy thriller, and that's a good description.

YOU: Have you noticed that there seem to be a lot of good movies around this summer?

SHE: Yes, I have. I read somewhere that movies are breaking all kinds of box office records this year and it's because there are so many lighthearted escape movies being produced. The studios are catching onto what people want to see.

YOU: Speaking of entertainment, have you been to any of the concerts at Levitt Pavilion?

SCENE 2. Telling a friend an interesting experience you have had

The same lunch date. Once again, things have slowed down. This time, after a moment's reflection, you come up with an interesting experience you had this week.

YOU: I had the most frustrating experience this week trying to keep an appointment I had for a job at New York Hospital. My train was fifteen minutes late getting into the city, which just barely left me enough time to make my appointment—if I had been able to get a cab right away, but I couldn't. I started off walking, hailed a cab going the wrong way, and got stuck in traffic. We inched up First Avenue, and I finally got out and ran the last two blocks—already fifteen minutes late. The worst was yet to come! I found the Payne Whitney Clinic all right, but nobody seemed to have heard of the doctor I was supposed to see. I kept running into open offices asking people if they knew where he was. Even the receptionist downstairs couldn't help. When I finally located him, he was busy and kept me waiting ten more minutes! At least I had a chance to catch my breath. Has anything like that ever happened to you?

SCENE 3. Introducing a current topic for discussion

The same lunch date. Pause in conversation.

YOU: What did you think about Joan Kennedy telling the press all her personal problems?

SHE: I thought it was brave of her to admit she was an alcoholic and was trying to overcome it. What was your reaction?

YOU: In a way it seemed like a publicity stunt. I don't mean she doesn't have a problem—I just don't see any reason for broadcasting it.

SHE: I still think it was a courageous thing to do.

YOU: To me it sounded like Betty Ford all over again. Maybe both of them are trying to make sure their husbands don't run for president. It must have been embarrassing for the families.

SHE: But it can't be a coincidence that two such prominent politicians' wives are coming up with the same problem in such a short period of time. I wouldn't like to take on a role like that.

YOU: Neither would I.

SCENE 4. Making a conversational connection

The same lunch date. Your friend has been telling you about a recent trip to Puerto Rico, where she attended a convention with her husband. Note that there is a wealth of possible connections from any reasonable topic or statement. In this case, possibilities include: "That reminds me of ... the time I was trying to speak Spanish to a Puerto Rican in New York; my one a.. J only visit to the Caribbean; the last convention I attended; the painting holiday my instructor conducted this summer which I'd like to have joined."

YOU: That makes me wish even more that I had been able to go on the painting holiday my watercolor instructor conducted in Puerto Rico this summer.

SHE: Oh, I think you really would have enjoyed it. If I could paint, I know I would have found a lot of subjects.

YOU: What was the most beautiful thing you saw?

SHE: It depends on whether you prefer beach scenes or city streets. I imagine Old San Juan would be the most interesting to paint.

YOU: My painting teacher must think so too. He has a studio in Old San Juan and spends part of the winter there every year.

ACT IV. INTRODUCTIONS

SCENE 1. Introducing two strangers to each other

You are the host at a small cocktail party. You have just greeted a new arrival and after a few minutes' conversation, introduce her to several other guests who are standing together.

YOU: I'd like you all to meet Betty Williams, who's just published her first novel. Betty, this is Nathan Walsh of Walsh Books; Evelyn King, a student at the University of Connecticut; and Jim Sims, assistant golf pro at the country club.

SCENE 2. Maintaining your composure when you forget someone's name

You are the hostess at a small cocktail party. You notice that two people are standing alone and decide to introduce them to each other.

YOU: Joan, there's someone over here I'd like to have you meet. I think you two would enjoy knowing each other. [*You have now approached the man standing alone, who happens to be a fairly good friend of yours and who looks relieved to see somebody coming.*] Hi! I'd like you to meet Joan Weber, who is just back from a summer in San Miguel. Joan, this is . . . oh, I'm so embarrassed! Would you believe I can't think of your name? Please forgive me.

Getting 7
beyond Small Talk

Some people are just naturally "up front"—open and direct, quick to relate to others at more than a superficial level.

But for most shy people it's very difficult to open up and reveal anything personal, likes and dislikes, feelings and opinions. Most shy people feel uncomfortable at the idea of telling a friend something good about themselves, accepting a compliment without denigrating themselves, or relating an embarrassing experience. They're likely to feel so self-conscious that they feel their opinions aren't worthwhile. They may not even feel that they *have* any opinions.

I can recall as a shy and awkward adolescent how extremely uncomfortable I felt if during a deadly pause in the conversation, on one of my rather infrequent dates, someone asked what I was thinking. I'd immediately freeze and be unable to think of anything but the fact that there was nothing on my mind. I could never name a favorite author, a favorite movie actor, or a favorite song; my mind would go blank if anyone asked. And I spent many frantic moments racking my brains to think of something—anything—that might be used to fill up a hole in the conversation.

As an only child, I grew up without learning how to relate easily to peers of the opposite sex (somehow girlfriends weren't a problem), and I also suffered from the excruciating disadvantage of being too smart for a girl. This became less of a problem after I went East to college, but even much later I continued to be shy—not only where small talk was concerned, but also about revealing much about myself. Perhaps I didn't know myself well enough to reveal me to anyone else. It has taken me a long time to learn to know and accept my own feelings and express them. Helping others to do this has helped me, too.

In moving beyond small talk to a more personal and meaningful level of communication, the most important rule to follow is: be yourself. A young divorced woman in one of my groups, discussing a forthcoming date with a man a few years older, recently remarked, "I can't decide whether to be the flirt or the sophisticate." When I asked why she didn't just be herself, she replied, "I guess I'm afraid he won't like me."

Most shy people are filled with insecurities about themselves and are uncertain of their own identities. One very attractive and articulate forty-year-old woman in a Shyness Clinic, divorced and supporting herself in a low-paying receptionist's job, said "I don't know how to present myself. I don't have a good job, I don't have any special talents or hobbies and all I was for fifteen years was a wife and mother. I feel like I'm nobody now." Many adolescents, especially those without clearly delineated career interests or special achievements, feel like "nobody." And many middle-aged women, who have spent most of their lives as wives and mothers, feel like nobody. Men are less likely to experience this feeling since they usually have a vocational identity that gives them some sense of self.

The woman I mentioned above was an avid beach-comber and camper, and during a group exercise in "telling about an interesting experience" described a summer she spent on a deserted farm in Vermont, without indoor plumbing or electricity, living pioneer-style with her two young children. "One of my biggest accomplishments was constructing a picnic table myself," she said, adding that she looked back on the summer as one of the most pleasant in her life and that she experienced all four seasons in the space of a few months: "We arrived in May, when it was still spring, enjoyed a beautiful Vermont summer and the spectacular fall foliage, and left in October after the first snow." She had had many other interesting experiences in her lifetime and was adept at relating them, yet frequently felt she had nothing to say.

Acceptance of your own experiences and feelings as valid and worthwhile (equally as much so as everybody else's) is a necessary step in the process of becoming an integrated, fully functioning person. Carl Rogers is the most eloquent spokesman I know for this point of view, and I urge you to read his books *On Becoming a Person* and *Becoming Partners* if you need encouragement in listening to and expressing your own feelings.

Naturally, learning to express yourself openly and directly does not mean expressing *everything*. Your experiences at the psychiatrist's or the gynecologist's offices, and certain other details of your personal life, may not be appropriate grist for any conceivable conversation. Some remarks, even though they are expressive of a real feeling, would be in poor taste anywhere; keep these to yourself.

Other topics would be inappropriate in casual situations but possibly appropriate in others. The details of your divorce seldom belong in a conversation with somebody you just met. Some people feel that the way to relate openly to others is to spill out a lot of personal information at the first meeting. Others behave this way out of nervousness. If you're in doubt about whether a certain topic or comment is in good taste, you're probably better off not saying it.

Occasionally you may encounter someone who has the bad taste to ask you about details of your personal life that you do not wish to discuss or to ask you for personal information about a mutual friend that you do not wish to reveal. In such situations I think it is best to state pleasantly but firmly that you don't feel comfortable discussing this.

It has been surprising to me to discover how very many people, both old and young, have supposedly intimate relationships with people they can't talk to.

An attractive young student in my University of Connecticut Shyness Clinic had a steady girlfriend, but the main reason he felt comfortable with her was that she did most of the talking. He explained that he could usually think of something to say in response to her comments, but couldn't introduce any topics of his own.

A married woman in her fifties complained that her husband wouldn't talk to her for more than five to ten minutes at a stretch. "After that, I can just see him pulling down a shade in his head," she commented. "Then he retreats behind a book or newspaper, and I know that's it for the evening."

In still other cases, married couples refrain from expressing their true feelings to one another because "it might hurt her feelings" or "it would only make him mad." Communication difficulties—or the lack of any communication at all—are a frequent complaint among the married couples I see.

A good many communication problems have assertive difficulties at their root. You may know how you feel but be afraid to state your feelings because you're afraid somebody won't like you or you will "make waves." In other cases you may not even be sure how you feel, which means you have to learn to respect and respond to your gut feelings. "My gut reactions are usually right," one client told me, "but I'm usually afraid to trust them."

Your feelings are *you*. Learn to respect them, and in doing so you will not only learn to respect yourself more but will also gradually arrive at a clear definition of who, and what, you are.

You can't go through life (happily, that is) trying to respond the way you think you should or the way somebody else thinks you should. Eventually your body will rebel and your repressed feelings may express themselves in the form of ulcers, colitis, or tension headaches. That is why assertive training plays such an important role in the treatment of such diverse problems as colitis, tension headaches, and agoraphobia.

Some people, especially men, are turned off by the phrase *assertive training*. One man I met at a cocktail party accused me of "teaching fighting." And the last man to whom I admitted an involvement with assertive training positively recoiled. "Women are too smart already," he said. "If they get any more assertive, there'll be no hope for men."

I feel that the real point of assertive training is learning to express your feelings openly and directly, when appropriate. It could be called "learning to communicate." Being assertive and open about your own feelings implies a willingness to be equally receptive to the feelings of others.

You must be able to listen as well as talk, and show by your responses that you understand and care.

On the other hand, too many people—especially women—think that the way to get along with everybody is to be a good listener, never disagree with someone else's opinion, and always put the other person's needs first.

The reason I am not stressing listening and responding here, to the same extent as expressing your own feelings, is that most shy people are already better listeners than talkers.

Act I. In the Beginning . . .

Scene 1. Telling a stranger you are shy

You are at a party where you don't know anyone and are feeling very self-conscious. Although your initial impulse is to nurse a drink in the corner by yourself, or try to maintain a façade to conceal your uneasiness, you decide to walk up to an attractive stranger and admit your shyness.

YOU: Hi, my name is Dick Sharp. I'm looking for advice on not looking as shy as I feel.

SHE: I'm Ellen Wayne. You don't look a bit shy, and you don't sound shy either. Are you really?

YOU: Yes, I put up a good front. But I had to force myself to walk over here, even though I wanted to meet you.

SHE: I know how you feel. It isn't easy to walk up to a stranger. But I'm glad you did.

YOU: So am I. I knew you looked like somebody I'd like to talk to.

Scene 2. Admitting you have a blushing problem

You have volunteered to carry out a special project at a local nature center. You enjoy the work, but for some reason you blush every time the director—an attractive man in his forties—comes into the room where you are working. He has never mentioned your blushing or done anything to embarrass you, and you haven't figured out why he affects you like this. You feel sure he must have noticed your problem. He has just come into the room and you are acutely conscious of a sudden rush of blood to your head.

YOU: Good morning, Phil.

HE: Good morning, May.

YOU: I can feel myself blushing again! Phil, this is so embarrassing! I can't explain it, but whenever you come in I find myself blushing. I'm sure you must have noticed.

HE: I've wondered if I was doing something to embarrass you.

YOU: No, it's just that I'm self-conscious. It happens with other people too and it never fails to embarrass me. I used to think I would outgrow it, but if anything, it's getting worse.

HE: Please don't worry about blushing in front of me. Now that we've talked about it, I hope it won't bother you as much.

YOU: I'm glad I brought it up. I feel better now.

SCENE 3. Politely declining unwanted advice

You are at a political reception where your husband, a young attorney running for public office, is the guest of honor. You have just been introduced to two older politicians and their wives. You consider yourself a private person and do not enjoy being in the spotlight, especially as a politician's wife, and you are tired of having people ask you the same questions.

OLDER POLITICIAN: Katherine, it's nice to meet you at last. We've been hoping you would take an active part in the campaign. Don't you like being a politician's wife?

YOU: Now that you mention it, I'll have to admit I'm not too comfortable with the role.

OLDER POLITICIAN'S WIFE: Peter needs your support, Katherine. I've always told Al that anything he wanted to do was fine with me—I'm behind him a hundred percent.

YOU: Of course Peter has my support, but I am an artist and have to keep a part of my life for myself. I'm sorry if this is upsetting to other people, but I feel this is something for the two of us to work out.

SCENE 4. Telling people that you like them

You are at a newcomers' party. You and your husband moved to town a few months ago after living in a different part of the country for ten years. You haven't felt comfortable with many of the couples you've met in Fairfield County. But you have seen Betty and Hal Hunt on several occasions and you both like them very much. Tonight you find yourself with Hal as your dinner partner.

YOU: Hal, this seems like a good time to tell you how much Joe and I have enjoyed meeting you and Betty. Both of us like both of you a lot.

HE: That is certainly a nice thing for you to say. Most people wouldn't—say it, I mean. Betty and I feel the same way about the two of you.

YOU: It seems so difficult for couples to make friends. Usually I like one of them but not both—or I like them but Joe doesn't—or he likes them and I don't. There are so many possible combinations.

HE: We've had exactly the same experience.

ACT II. AS TIME GOES BY

SCENE 1. Disagreeing with a friend on a matter of taste

A department store. You are shopping with a friend. She has made a special point of wanting to show you a chess set she is contemplating buying. It is very expensive and doesn't appeal to you at all.

SHE: Oh, I'm so glad to get a chance to show you this chess set! Isn't it terrific-looking?

YOU: It's very interesting.

SHE: Don't you just *love* it?

YOU: I don't feel as enthusiastic as you do about it. It isn't something I would choose myself. But tastes differ so much, there's no reason why we should like all of the same things.

SHE: I'm disappointed. I hoped you would like it too. Now I'm wondering if I should buy it.

YOU: If you like it a lot, then I think you should buy it. Your own taste is what's important.

SCENE 2. Telling a friend something good about yourself

A department store. You are in the sportswear department looking at fall blazers when you recognize a friend at an adjacent display. You are delighted to see her because something very pleasant has just happened to you, and you have been wishing there was someone you could share it with.

YOU: Joan, I'm so glad to see you. Something just happened that I really wanted to tell a friend about.

SHE: That sounds exciting. What?

YOU: You probably remember that I've been doing the publicity for the photography club.

SHE: Yes, and I've seen several of your things in the paper lately.

YOU: I *have* gotten a lot of coverage lately. That leads up to what I wanted to tell you. I just bumped into the president of the photography club upstairs. He told me I've been doing such a terrific job that he has recommended me for a freelance publicity job for the Photo Shop.

SHE: I'm impressed! And glad for you. I can see why you feel good about all of that.

SCENE 3. Introducing an experience of your own when a friend is dominating the conversation

A cafeteria. You are having a cup of coffee with a friend. You had been looking forward to talking with him, but after half an hour you realize that this is a monologue, not a conversation. After being polite and nonassertive for longer than you want to be, you decide to introduce a topic of conversation of your own.

YOU: What you've been saying reminds me of a similar problem I'm having right now. I'd like to tell you about it.

HE: As I was saying, my boss has been impossible lately. He expects me to work late every night, and it's cutting into my social life.

YOU: That must be creating a difficult situation for you. But now it's my turn to tell you about *my* problem!

HE: I guess you're right.

SCENE 4. Telling a good friend that something she did bothered you

A restaurant. You are having lunch with a friend. As usual, she was almost twenty minutes late. This has annoyed you each time it happened, but you haven't spoken up. This time you decide to express your feelings.

YOU: Jane, there's something we really have to talk about.

SHE: What's that?

YOU: It really bothers me that you are late so often. I could understand if it happened once, but it's every time we get together.

SHE: I've always had trouble getting places on time. It's just the way I am.

YOU: You don't have to stay that way. It really irritates me, Jane. It makes me feel that you consider my time of no value, and I resent that.

SHE: I'm sorry. I didn't realize how you felt. I'll make sure I am prompt next time.

8

How to Ask for a Date

For most of my shy clients and students, inviting someone to do something, even a person of the same sex, is a very frightening prospect. Sometimes I ask them whether they're more afraid the person will say no—or that they'll say yes.

Mary, a fifty-year-old woman in an assertive training group, came into a session one evening and announced that she had a problem she hadn't mentioned yet, but had discussed with her psychiatrist. She'd told the psychiatrist that if she brought up the problem in assertive training, I would make her act it out. Then she explained the problem: She was literally petrified at the thought of asking a friend to have lunch with her. She felt certain nobody would want to.

Mary was right about one thing. I did "make her act it out," but only after the group discussed it and assured her that in all probability her invitation would be welcome, and only after several group members, including me, had acted out the situation first, to show Mary exactly what to say.

She was wrong about her second and third points—that she couldn't act it out and that she couldn't ask an acquaintance to lunch. She *did* act it out—haltingly and very self-consciously at first, but after several repetitions and much encouragement from the group, she began to feel more self-confident.

At the following week's meeting Mary announced jubilantly that she had invited a friend to lunch, that the conversation had gone exactly as we'd rehearsed it, and that they had a lunch date for the coming Monday. The most difficult part of the experience, she said, was getting herself to do it. She'd put off the call again and again, and finally did it the day before the group meeting. (One very beneficial aspect of the group experience is the feeling that you must go through with your project because the group expects it.) "I couldn't come in tonight and say I hadn't done it," Mary reported. "So I just had to call." I've heard variations on that theme many times.

When it comes to asking a person of the opposite sex for a date, the shy person usually goes through untold agonies. Most of us can recall having these feelings in adolescence; hardly anyone escapes them entirely during that painful phase of life. But most often the extreme self-consciousness of adolescence has begun to taper off by the end of high school. One man who recalled being extremely shy in high school told me that, knowing he was going to have to earn his way through college, he took stock of himself and realized that he could never achieve his goal if he continued to let shyness dominate his life. He determined to act differently and was able to do so.

However, many people who realize that their shyness is

a liability are unable to do anything about it on their own. I worked for months in individual therapy with one college student, aged twenty-three, who had never had a date in his life.

Week after week we rehearsed conversations and invitations, and week after week I desensitized him to various situations involving interactions with the opposite sex. His greatest fear was not being able to keep a conversation going, though he was a highly intelligent young man with good conversational ability and a wide range of general information. Eventually he was able to ask a girl for a date, but this milestone took months to accomplish.

Usually progress is faster. Another student of about the same age came to me with similar apprehensions. He had dated in the past, but when he first consulted me was not dating at all. He was leading an isolated life, living away from his family and having little contact with anyone his own age. He was working at various part-time jobs while taking the college courses he needed to complete his degree. Between sessions with me he found few opportunities to converse with anyone else. I used the sessions mainly as conversational practice for him, encouraging him to bring up topics for discussion and to gain more confidence in relating interesting events that occurred during the week. I also desensitized him to certain interpersonal situations and we discussed the specific difficulties he was having in meeting and conversing with others. After several months he was dating regularly without anxiety. Bruce felt that the conversational practice he gained in talking to me was the most important factor in overcoming his shyness.

Jim, a college graduate in his twenties, employed by a large corporation, had not asked a girl for a date in over a year when he joined one of my Shyness Clinics. He participated in group desensitization sessions and repeatedly practiced asking the girls in the clinic for dates. At the end of the clinic he had had three dates and was feeling much better about himself. Jim said that "the permission to ask people out" he gained from my encouragement and from the group practice helped him the most. Several months after the clinic ended, Jim asked one of the girls in the group for a date—and she accepted.

Another member of the same group had a steady girlfriend (he reported that she did most of the talking) but he had few other friends. After a few sessions involving practice invitations, he succeeded in asking a classmate to play paddle tennis with him. Matt was very pleased with this accomplishment.

Like most other shy people, Matt had not been in the habit of taking the initiative himself. One of the first things shy people need to learn is that they must be willing to make the first move toward another person.

Some shy people find it easier to make their first invitational efforts by phone. Others feel less anxiety if they do their asking in person. You should decide which approach is easier for you, and then do it the easy way first.

When asking for a date by phone, here are a few simple rules to follow:

1. Begin by saying "May I please speak to Ellen?" Or, questioningly, "Ellen?" Don't say "Who's this?"
2. State your name clearly. Unless you know the person well or have some other reason for being absolutely certain you will be recognized by your voice or by your first name, use your first *and* last name.
3. If there is a reasonable chance that the person may not remember your name, identify yourself further by briefly stating where you met: "I sit next to you in

physics class" or "We met at the Players Tavern last week." Don't say "Do you remember me?" or "You may not remember me, but . . ."

Answering the phone

Figuring out what to say when you telephone someone is reasonably straightforward: "May I speak to Eleanor Williams, please?"

If you happen to be Eleanor Williams, deciding what to say is a little more difficult. One of my favorite short pieces by E. B. White concerns this dilemma.

Commenting on a newspaper query, "What is the correct response when someone calls you on the telephone and asks for you by name?," he has the following to say:

> Not only is there no "correct" response when this disagreeable thing happens, but there is no real response possible—in the true sense of the word. Anything you say is a makeshift. Hundreds of "responses" have been tried by millions of phone users; every one has proved either evasive or ridiculous or rude.
>
> Let us say your name is Brinckerhoff. The phone rings and you answer it and a voice says, "I would like to speak to Mr. Brinckerhoff, please." You are in an impossible situation. You can say, "This is I," and be put down for a purist or a poseur. Or you can say, "This is me," and be taken for a tough. Or, rather desperately, you can reply, "This is he," or "This is Brinckerhoff," or "This is Mr. Brinckerhoff," referring to yourself grandiloquently in the third person, in the manner of dictators and kings. Believe us, when a man starts referring to himself in the third person, the end of the good life is not far off. To the listener you sound either downright silly or deliberately vainglorious. Your "response" has a slightly moldy, undemocratic sound, as when, in the presence of a servant, you refer to your wife as "Mrs. Brinckerhoff" instead of as "Esther."

Now, suppose you go off on an entirely different tack when the phone rings and someone asks for you by name. Suppose you say, with forced cheeriness, "Speaking!" What a pitiful attempt! The word has hardly rolled off your tongue when it becomes meaningless, for you are no longer speaking but are listening—listening, and hoping against hope that it isn't somebody you can't stand. Or let's take a few other conventional "responses" and see how miserably they fail:

VOICE: I would like to speak to Mr. Brinckerhoff, please."
RESPONSE: "You are." This is too rude, too familiar.
VOICE: "I would like to speak to Mr. Brinckerhoff, please."
RESPONSE: "Why?" This is evasive, prying.
VOICE: "I would like to speak to Mr. Brinckerhoff, please."
RESPONSE: "Go ahead!" Peremptory, unfriendly.

No, there is no "correct" response in this situation. There is no response that is anything but discouraging. It is the most difficult and disturbing phase of one's telephonic life. Unquestionably it was not foreseen by Mr. Bell when he was so blithely tinkering with his little magnets and diaphragms. If only a voice could have whispered, "I would like to speak to Mr. Alexander Graham Bell, please," how much that might have saved the world! Bell would have laid down his tools with a tired sigh, a man who knew when he was licked.*

If E. B. White, one of the world's most articulate individuals, has been unable to resolve this thorny problem, it would be presumptuous of me to think that I could do so. And in reading the scripts I have provided to assist the timid, it will be obvious that I have merely sidestepped the question. I've assumed that you'll find it appropriate in most sit-

* "Answers to Hard Questions," in *The Second Tree from the Corner*, New York: Harper & Row, 1935, pp. 91–92.

uations to reply "This is Edgar," providing of course that Edgar happens to be your first name. Since White didn't give us a first name for Brinckerhoff, apparently this didn't occur to him as a possible solution, and in some cases it clearly wouldn't work out. If the first-name response doesn't seem suitable, then you are on your own: White has detailed a number of suggestions which can be considered, and perhaps discarded, on their relative merits.

What About a Woman Asking a Man for a Date?

I am frequently asked that question. Personally, I'd like to think that the old rules had changed sufficiently so that we are all adults now, and a man can ask a woman out if he feels like it—and a woman can ask a man out if *she* feels like it. This is what I'd like to think, but not what I do think.

Certainly in an ongoing relationship the woman should be just as free to initiate telephone calls, invitations, and sex as the man, in my opinion.

If you are just starting or hoping to get a relationship going, I still think that *ideally* this equality should prevail, but I don't think it does. As one divorced woman college professor commented, "If you call a guy to get together, my experience is that their reaction is polite to contemptuous, but never pleased. It's the same old 1950s rules of the game: A woman does not call and does not initiate."

There are still plenty of men around who feel that way—no doubt a majority of them. And if a woman is interested in a man who does, then she would be unwise to come on too strong.

I would like to think that if a man is that constrained by traditional sex-role expectations, he isn't a man I could ever be interested in anyway—so I would have nothing to lose by inviting him to do something if I felt like it. Yet I know that most of the time I would not act on that particular conviction because the response would be so unpredictable that I might be afraid of rocking the boat.

This is another question that must be decided on the basis of good taste and good judgment as to what is appropriate or acceptable in a particular situation.

If the Answer is No

You'll notice that I have written the scripts from an optimistic point of view, assuming that your invitation will be accepted. I don't see any point in practicing for rejection. Early in my career I worked with one student who feared rejection, and I role-played situations with him in which the girl did say no. But this was too discouraging for him, so I discontinued it.

Now in discussing invitations with shy clients I try to allay such anxieties by pointing out that the worst that can happen is that the person will say no; that yes is a more probable outcome; and that if occasionally somebody does say no, it isn't the end of the world.

When a client gets up the courage to issue an invitation and is refused, I concentrate on the positive aspect of the situation: "It's great that you asked, and the result is less important than the fact that you tried. Next time it will be easier." You should give yourself the same kind of positive encouragement if you encounter a no.

In case of repeated rejections, the problem becomes much more difficult. Several failures can really set a shy person back. I try to prevent such an occurrence by discussing the question of whom to invite. In the beginning it is more important to get some positive results and some dating experience than it is to score with the most popular person in town. Try someone who is likely to be a little more available.

Much faulty communication centers around issuing

and receiving invitations. It is important to be specific. Say "Would you like to see *Heaven Can Wait* at the Avon tonight?" or "I was wondering if you'd like to go out and eat Chinese food on Friday," not "Are you busy Saturday?" or "What are you doing tonight?" And don't be apologetic; don't say "If you're not doing anything, do you want to go to the movies with me?"

In addition to a specific answer to this invitation, you may be looking for some more general information as well. You'd like to know whether the person is interested in going out with you some other time. This is not always made clear.

When a shy person hears "No," he or she may not hear what follows, even though it may be entirely legitimate. "I'm busy tonight" or "I'm sorry, I can't make it this time" usually means exactly that. But most shy people are unlikely to come back with "How about next weekend then?" or "Would you like to go out some other time?" After you have gained a little self-confidence, I think you *will* be able to do this—unless you feel absolutely certain from the response you received that this person doesn't want to go out with you.

When You're Invited

If you are on the receiving end of an invitation and you cannot accept it but would like to, be sure to make that clear. Say "I'm busy tonight but I'd love to do it some other time," or "Please call me again," or "I'm really sorry that I can't make it this time. How about a rain check?" With a response like this, the other person will feel encouraged to ask you another time.

I am often asked what to do if you don't want to go out with that person any other time either. The first time, I think it is kinder to say "Thanks, but I'm afraid I can't." (Remember that you do not need an excuse to decline an invitation.)

I would probably give a similar response on the second, possibly even the third invitation. But if the other person persists, you may as well come out with your feelings directly with as much tact as possible. You might say something like "You're nice to ask me, but I'd rather not."

It is essential to learn to say no to invitations you don't want to accept. Otherwise, your social life is entirely out of your control.

ACT I. DIAL TONE

SCENE 1. Calling up a classmate, same sex, to make a date

VOICE: Hello.

YOU: Hello. May I speak to Lila, please?

VOICE: This is Lila.

YOU: This is Jenny Donaldson. Do you feel like going with me to the Spanish party at school tonight?

VOICE: Oh, I'm glad you called, Jenny. I'd thought of going, but didn't want to go alone. I'd like to go with you.

YOU: I have a car tonight, so I can come by and pick you up. I know you don't live far from campus. Where's your house exactly?

VOICE: It's right on Coley Road, the fourth house from the corner. Number twenty-six. It's white with black shutters.

YOU: I'll pick you up about eight. See you then.

SCENE 2. Calling a classmate, opposite sex, to make a date

VOICE: Hello.

YOU: Hello, may I speak to Lila, please?

VOICE: This is Lila.

YOU: This is Jerry Donaldson. Would you like to go with me to the beer fest at school tonight? I went to one earlier in the year, and it was a lot of fun.

VOICE: Thanks, Jerry. I'd like to. I noticed the signs around campus. What time does it start?

YOU: It starts at eight, but I think nine would be a better time to get there. I'll pick you up around eight forty-five.

VOICE: That's fine with me. Do you know where I live?

YOU: It's near campus, isn't it? But I don't know the exact address.

VOICE: Number Twenty-six Coley Road, the fourth house in from the corner. It's white with black shutters.

YOU: Great, I'll see you about eight forty-five.

SCENE 3. Calling someone you've met at a party, same sex, to make a date

VOICE: Hello.

YOU: May I speak to Steve Miller, please?

VOICE: This is Steve.

YOU: Steve, this is Patrick Evans. I'm calling to follow up on our conversation at the Thompsons' party last weekend—we were talking about playing golf. How about getting together tomorrow evening after work?

VOICE: That sounds like a good idea. I'd like to. What time can you get to Oak Hills?

YOU: I can make it by five-thirty. Is that good for you?

VOICE: Yes, that's fine.

YOU: I'll meet you at five-thirty, then.

SCENE 4. Calling someone you've met at a party, opposite sex, to make a date

VOICE: Hello.

YOU: May I please speak to Stephanie Miller?

VOICE: This is Stephanie.

YOU: Stephanie, this is Patrick Evans. We were talking at Joe Thompson's party last weekend.

VOICE: I remember. You just moved here from the West Coast.

YOU: Yes, that's right. I called to ask if you'd like to go with me to see the play at the Westport Country Playhouse tomorrow evening.

VOICE: I'd love to. The newspaper reviews were really good.
YOU: The play starts at eight-thirty. Where do you live?
VOICE: On Cove Drive in Stamford—the second house in from the Post Road. You'll see our name on the mailbox, and the house is red.
YOU: I'll stop by for you about seven-thirty.
VOICE: Fine. I'll see you then.

SCENE 5. Calling someone you don't know to arrange to play tennis together

VOICE: Hello.
YOU: Hello, may I speak to Evelyn Hayes, please?
VOICE: This is Evelyn.
YOU: This is Connie Archer. I'm calling about tennis. I saw your name on the list at the Three Seasons Tennis Club, and wondered if we could set up a game.
VOICE: Yes, I'd like to. I just hope you're not too good for me. How well do you play?
YOU: I'm a B player.
VOICE: That sounds good. When's a convenient time for you?
YOU: How about Friday at two?
VOICE: That's fine. I'll meet you there.

SCENE 6. Calling someone you know only vaguely to make a tennis date

VOICE: Hello.
YOU: May I speak to Joan, please?
VOICE: This is Joan.
YOU: This is Susan O'Rourke.
VOICE: Susan who?
YOU: Susan O'Rourke. We belong to the same country club, and I've seen you play tennis there. Would you like to play with me sometime, now that the weather is nice?
VOICE: Yes, I'd like to. I've been playing indoors and can't wait to get outside.

YOU: Could you make it at three either Thursday or Friday?

VOICE: Thursday would be fine with me. I'll meet you at the court at three o'clock.

YOU: I'll look forward to it.

SCENE 7. Calling a friend of a friend to make a date

VOICE: Hello.

YOU: May I speak to Bertha Rush, please?

VOICE: This is Bertha.

YOU: My name is George Hamilton. Al Jamison suggested I call you—he's my roommate at Ohio State. He told me you were moving to New Canaan and he thought we'd have a lot in common. Could we get together some evening soon for a drink?

VOICE: That sounds like fun. I haven't seen George for over a year and I'd really like to hear all about him. We've been good friends since eighth grade!

YOU: Then all we need to do is figure out a convenient time. How about tonight?

VOICE: That's fine with me.

YOU: I'll pick you up about nine o'clock. Where is Valley Road exactly?

VOICE: It goes off Silvermine, if you know where that is.

YOU: Yes, I do.

VOICE: My house is on the left, number ten.

YOU: Great. I'll see you at nine.

VOICE: I'll be ready.

ACT II. APPEARING IN PERSON

SCENE 1. Asking an acquaintance you encounter casually to have tea with you

The linen department of Bloomingdale's, where a half-yearly white sale is in progress. A clerk is writing up the new towels you have selected for the children's bathroom when you hear a

familiar voice speaking to the salesperson at an adjacent cash register. You look up and recognize a woman you have worked with on several PTA committees. She is someone you like and would enjoy knowing better. You feel awkward about taking the initiative but remind yourself that you must do so if you want to expand your social horizons.

YOU: Sue, it's nice to see you. Now that school is out, I don't see anybody but my children!

SHE: I know exactly what you mean. With them home all day every day, it's a whole new ball game.

YOU: I was thinking of having a cup of tea. Do you have time to join me?

SHE: Thanks. That sounds like a good idea. Shopping for an hour or two is about all I can take. Do you mind if I buy these sheets first? I know I won't want to come back later.

YOU: I don't mind at all. I'll wait for you over in the housewares department.

SCENE 2. Asking someone you work with, same sex, to have lunch with you

A busy office. It is midmorning. You are delivering copy for a new ad to the advertising manager and stop for a moment to speak to her assistant.

YOU: Would you like to go out for lunch today, Teresa?

SHE: Yes, I'd like to. Where shall we go?

YOU: How about the steak house across the street? Their teriaki burgers are good and the service is fast. They have different kinds of burgers, and a salad bar and a few other things. Or maybe you've been there?

SHE: No, I haven't. It sounds good. What time would you like to go?

YOU: How about twelve thirty? I'll meet you in the lobby.

SHE: Okay, I'll see you then.

SCENE 3. Asking someone you work with, opposite sex, to have lunch with you

*The same setting as Scene 2, but this time the assistant adver-
tising manager is male. You'd like to know him better and wish
he would ask you to lunch. But since he hasn't, you remind
yourself that you have a perfectly legitimate reason for asking
him.*

YOU: I've been wanting to talk to you about the new advertising campaign, Terry. Could we get together for
lunch soon?

HE: That sounds like a fine idea, How about today?

YOU: That would be great.

HE: Would twelve-thirty be convenient for you?

YOU: Yes, that's perfect. Have you tried the steak house
across the street? Or do you have a better idea?

HE: I'm with you. Why don't we meet at twelve-thirty in
the lobby?

YOU: Good, I'll see you then.

SCENE 4. Asking someone you see casually, but regularly, for a date

*McDonald's, midafternoon. Things are quiet, with only a few
people standing waiting for orders. You planned your arrival to
coincide with slow time, since you are hoping to get a chance
to ask one of the waitresses for a date. You've already discovered that you can't do it when the place is crowded.*

YOU: Hi, Tina. How are things going today?

SHE: Hectic as usual. But right now we're getting a breather.
Not too many people eat lunch at three o'clock. What
would you like?

YOU: Now that you mention it, I didn't come to eat. I came
to ask you for a date. How about going with me to see
Grease this weekend?

SHE: I'd like to, but I'm working until nine o'clock Saturday and Sunday both. Do you mind going to the late
show?

YOU: That's what I had in mind anyway. It starts at ten on
Saturday. Could you be ready in time for that?

SHE: Yes. I'll want to go home and change, but I don't live far from here. Could you pick me up at nine-thirty? I live at twenty-four Queens Highway.

YOU: Fine, I'll see you at nine-thirty Saturday.

SCENE 5. Asking someone you've just met, same sex, for a telephone number

A business seminar. You have been seated next to a young man about your own age and have conversed with him very enjoyably during the day.

YOU: Dick, I've enjoyed talking with you today. Why don't we get together for lunch some day soon?

HE: I'd like that. I've enjoyed our conversation too.

YOU: What's your number? I'll give you a ring soon.

HE: Here's my card.

YOU: Thanks. I'll be in touch in a few days.

SCENE 6. Asking someone you've just met, opposite sex, for a telephone number

A singles party. You have spent a good part of the evening dancing with an attractive blonde. You'd like to see her again and wonder how she feels about you. You remind yourself that she's been acting interested—so she probably is.

YOU: Sally, it's been a great evening. I'd like to see you again soon. What's your phone number?

SHE: It's 335-4321.

YOU: Since we both like country music, I'm going to check on what's coming up in the area in that department. I think I read that the Apple Country String Band will be in Stamford soon.

SHE: I'd like to hear them.

YOU: I'll see what I can find out and call you tomorrow. Will you be home in the evening?

SHE: Yes, I'll be there.

Act III. Come On Over to My House

Scene 1. Calling a new neighbor to invite her for coffee

VOICE: Hello.

  YOU: May I speak to Christine Walters, please?

VOICE: This is Christine Walters.

  YOU: My name is Ava Olson. I called to welcome you to the neighborhood. I've tried to stop by and introduce myself, but haven't found you at home. Could you come over for coffee tomorrow?

VOICE: Thank you very much. I'd like to meet you. It's nice to have a friendly neighbor.

  YOU: Could you come about ten? I'll invite a few other neighbors.

VOICE: Thanks again, Ava. I'll look forward to seeing you at ten tomorrow.

Scene 2. Calling a new friend to invite her to a dinner party at your house

VOICE: Hello.

  YOU: Frances?

VOICE: Yes, this is Frances.

  YOU: This is Edwina Smythe. We're having a few people over to dinner next Friday before the dance at the club and wondered if you and Bill could come.

VOICE: Oh, that sounds very nice, Edwina. We'd like to. It was such fun talking to you both last weekend.

  YOU: We'll look forward to seeing you about seven-thirty, then.

VOICE: Thank you, Edwina. We'll be there.

Scene 3. Inviting someone at work to a cocktail party

An advertising agency where you are a layout artist. You stop by the office of one of the junior account executives and pause by the door.

  YOU: Hi, Jim. I'm having a few people over for cocktails to-morrow about five. Can you come?

HE: That's nice of you, Doris. It sounds fine. I'll be there. What's your address?

YOU: I live on Glenbrook road in the new condominium— number fifty-three. I'll see you about five tomorrow, then.

HE: Thanks, Doris. I'll look forward to seeing you tomorrow.

How to Speak Up 9 in a Group

Speaking up in a group situation is a nightmare for most shy people. The feeling that you are the center of attention, the fear of making a mistake or sounding stupid, and the butterflies and blushes that accompany these emotions are frequently enough to make a shy person want to rush for the nearest exit.

"I never speak up in class," one young student declared. "Every time I go to class I wonder how I can avoid getting called on. I wouldn't think of volunteering either a question or an answer."

Surprising as it may seem, I have worked with several law students with this complaint: they were terrified of speaking up in class. Some professors make the situation worse by ridiculing a student who asks a question the professor considers elementary or who gives an answer that is not exactly what the professor had in mind. Such ridicule is devastating for anyone, especially a shy person.

But even if the professor is friendly, overcoming old habits of reticence is not easy. It requires a determined effort on your part—particularly the first few times.

One of my clients, someone I worked with both individually and in a group, had always been so anxious in group situations and so afraid of saying the wrong thing in class that she had virtually no energy left over for the intellectual task at hand. As a result, she did very poorly in school and considered herself stupid. After more than a year of therapy she decided to go back to school, and enrolled in a community college class in economics. She took out several textbooks on the subject from the library and started reading them before the course began. On the first night of class she felt entirely at ease with the subject matter, easily followed what the instructor was saying, and knew the answer to every question he asked.

But she saw herself continuing her old behavior pattern. Each time the instructor asked a question and Elise knew the answer but did not volunteer, she became increasingly disgusted with herself. Finally she said to herself: "If you don't speak up and answer the next question, you will have wasted all that time and energy studying." She forced herself to volunteer an answer to the next question and answered another before the end of the class. She left feeling very pleased with what she had accomplished.

Obviously, classroom situations are not the only occasions that involve fear of speaking up in a group. One housewife in her fifties admitted that she felt very ill at ease in any group of more than six people: "Every time I go to a lecture I can think of questions I want to ask, but I never ask them." She recalled how, as a budding child actress, she was taken to Hollywood for an audition and promptly went blank when her turn came. When in a group situation, conscious of feeling onstage again, she frequently remembered that experience.

"I can usually get along all right talking to one other person," another forty-year-old woman explained, "but just let me get in a group of people and my mind goes blank. I can't think of a single thing to say. I feel so inferior because of this. Here I am the mother of five children, yet I can't even function socially. My oldest daughter wants to have a big wedding when she graduates from law school, but I don't think I can face it. I just can't imagine being able to talk to all those people. When I was asked to preside at a church meeting recently, I started shaking just at the thought of it."

A student in his twenties said that one of the prospects he dreaded most was being asked to serve as best man at a friend's wedding—because he would be expected to toast the bride and goom. One of the group members suggested that he find a book that would help him compose an appropriate toast. He did so, and practiced delivering it at the next meeting to prepare for this eventuality. As far as I know, it hasn't happened yet, but hopefully he will be able to handle the situation if it does occur.

Obviously, making a toast at a wedding, introducing a visiting lecturer, or even serving as club treasurer and making reports at club meetings are all getting into the sphere of public speaking. I am not going to go very far in this book with the problems encountered in formal speeches and lectures, because it is such a big topic and in some ways a separate one. Many people who are not shy in most situations suffer excruciating anxiety if they must speak in public. Some well-known actors and actresses, opera singers and other successful performers experience stage fright before every curtain. Many of them could be helped by desensitization, as the technique is applicable to any difficulty where fear or anxiety is the underlying problem. If you must deliver a speech or lecture, you can use the same techniques you have mastered for handling social situations to help allay your anxieties.

ACT I. FORMALLY SPEAKING

SCENE 1. Asking the professor to explain something you didn't understand in class

A college class in computer programming with about twenty-five students present. You are sitting in the back row. The professor has just finished explaining the algebraic proof for a FORTRAN program. You have the feeling that you are missing some essential piece of information, and you know that if you don't speak up you will continue to be hopelessly confused.

YOU: Professor Jackson, I don't understand this proof. Could you please explain it again?

PROFESSOR: What is it you don't understand?

YOU: I just don't understand any of it. Could you explain it more slowly?

PROFESSOR: I'm not teaching elementary algebra here. You're supposed to know that before you get into this class.

YOU: I consider myself competent in elementary algebra, but this proof is very involved. I would appreciate it if you would explain it again.

PROFESSOR: Is there anyone else in the group who needs help with this equation?

CLASS [Chorus]: Yes!

PROFESSOR: Very well. I'll go through it again.

SCENE 2. Answering a direct question in class

A college class in economics, with about fifteen students present. This particular professor has a habit of calling on randomly selected students. Today you happen to be the student se-

lected. If you do not know the answer, look directly at the professor and say you don't know.

> PROFESSOR: What happens to the level of investment when the interest rate goes up, Gene?
>
> YOU: It goes down.
>
> PROFESSOR: Why?
>
> YOU: Because it costs more to borrow money and the opportunity cost is higher. The present value of the future stream of income is lower, because the marginal efficiency of capital is lower.
>
> PROFESSOR: Very good, Gene. Just one more point. Can you explain why the marginal efficiency goes down?
>
> YOU: No, I'm sorry. I don't know.

SCENE 3. Giving a brief presentation in class

A speech class. There are about ten students present. Today it is your turn to make a brief presentation. The topic you have chosen is shyness.

> YOU: I'm going to talk to you today about shyness. This is a topic of which I have firsthand knowledge, since I've been shy all my life and have been covering it up successfully most of the time. Usually I don't say anything about being shy. I try to act as if I were not shy. I force myself to talk to strangers and speak up in class, but inside I'm dying. I probably look and sound perfectly calm. But the truth of the matter is that I'm scared to death.
>
> I used to think that no one else in the world felt the way I did. Then I read a book by Philip Zimbardo, a California psychologist, called *Shyness*—and I discovered that lots of other people, 40 percent according to Zimbardo, consider themselves shy. Since reading his book I have found the courage to mention my shyness to a few of my friends—and I found out that some of *them* feel shy too. It's made me feel better to know I am not alone, and I'm trying very hard to overcome my

shyness, because I find that it gets in my way in social situations and because I realize now that it's not something I just have to live with.

SCENE 4. Asking a question at a public lecture

A school auditorium. You are attending a lecture on drug problems among teenagers given by a Colorado psychologist, Dr. Everett Turner. It is now time for the question-and-answer period. Ordinarily, you would think of several questions you wanted to ask and then rationalize explanations for not asking them. This time you decide to go ahead and ask your question.

YOU: Dr. Turner, you referred to angel dust or PCP as the LSD of the seventies. Could you elaborate on that point?

HE: Yes. PCP is the most dangerous drug to hit the streets since LSD. Chronic exposure produces loss of memory, changes in personality, depression, and sometimes suicidal and homicidal tendencies. Even a single use of the drug can lead to bizarre or violent behavior.

YOU: How long do these effects last?

HE: Some symptoms persist for months or years. After chronic exposure, it's possible a person may never again be normal.

YOU: I don't understand how this drug suddenly became so popular.

HE: It's easier and cheaper to get than any other drug except marijuana. Pushers are making big money from it. It can be manufactured fairly easily. It may be a powder, a leaf mixture, a tablet, or a liquid. It can be smoked with marijuana or injected.

YOU: How can the use of this drug be stopped?

HE: By educating young people about the danger. This drug is so potent that it shouldn't be tried even once.

SCENE 5. Being put on the spot as an instant celebrity

A school auditorium. You are attending a lecture on herb gardening given by a member of the garden club you regularly at-

tend. *During the question-and-answer period following the lecture, a member of the audience asks the speaker if watercress can be grown indoors. This happens to be your specialty and you know from garden club discussions that the speaker has relatively little experience or knowledge of it. To your horror, you hear the speaker saying "I'm not an expert on growing watercress indoors, but fortunately there is someone with us tonight who is. Dorcas, could you tell us about your experience with this?"*

You have been transformed from anonymous listener to instant expert. Although you fervently wish you had stayed home, you take a deep breath and slowly rise to the occasion. You speak slowly and distinctly, comforted by the knowledge that you do know more about this particular topic than anyone else in the room.

YOU: Yes, I'll be glad to tell you what I can. I've been a watercress enthusiast for a long time and used to go back to my parents' house in the country regularly to collect watercress. I had never thought of trying to grow it indoors because several gardening experts told me it was difficult or impossible to do. I'm glad to report that they're wrong. A dozen clay pots, or fewer if you don't use a lot of watercress, can provide you with a continuous supply during the winter.

QUESTIONER: What kind of pots do you recommend?

YOU: I use eight-inch clay bulb pans, which are shorter and wider than standard pots. You need a few clay shards in the bottom of each pot, an inch of aquarium charcoal, and enough fertile, sandy soil to fill the pots. The pots are set in four-inch metal pans which you keep full of water.

QUESTIONER: Do you use cuttings or seeds?

YOU: It's possible to use either, but cuttings are much faster. I take three-inch cuttings from the tops of watercress plants from the grocery store, poke holes in the soil with a pencil, and stick the cuttings into the holes about an inch deep. About six to eight cuttings can fit into each pot.

QUESTIONER: Do they require a lot of sun?
YOU: Yes, a sunny windowsill is the best location.

ACT II. ON THE SOCIAL SCENE

SCENE 1. Relating an interesting experience to a group of friends

You are telling several friends about an interesting experience you had recently. Everyone is listening to your story and you have the feeling that the spotlight is on you.

YOU: Something happened to me Friday night that was so funny I really have to share it with you. Ed and I went out to dinner at Manero's, and it was very crowded when we got there. They showed us to a table right by the entrance to the kitchen. I had the feeling I wasn't going to like it, but as usual I didn't say anything. I tried to tell myself it would be all right. But after we'd been sitting there a few minutes it was really bothering me. The waiters were constantly rushing back and forth right by me, and it was so noisy and distracting that we could barely conduct a conversation. I suggested to Ed that he ask for a different table, but he said it was too late—we should have asked when we first came in. So of course I didn't say anything more, even though I knew at that point it was definitely going to ruin my evening.

You won't believe what happened a few minutes later. A waiter came hurrying past and spilled a whole basket of rolls in my lap! I just sat there staring at them. That's the last time I am going to let anybody make me sit by the kitchen door.

SCENE 2. Being questioned by several people about a recent experience

The pub in a college campus center. It is the week after spring vacation, which you spent with a college friend in St. Thomas. the two of you took a charter flight to the island and took a chance on finding accommodations. Now everyone wants to know what the experience was like.

ONE OF THEM: Tell us about St. Thomas, Bob! You and Stan must have had a better vacation than anyone.

YOU: It was super. We found a double room in a little boarding house near the center of Charlotte Amalie. It was only seven dollars a night apiece and breakfast came with the deal.

ONE OF THEM: How did you ever find it?

YOU: We just got off the plane, took a cab into town, and started walking around looking for a cheap place to stay.

ONE OF THEM: What about the beach? Is there a beach right in town?

YOU: We usually took a cab to the other side of the island to a deserted beach—I never saw such a beautiful spot anyplace. The ocean is a different color in the Caribbean. It was my first trip down there, but for sure it won't be my last.

ONE OF THEM: Did you talk to any of the natives?

YOU: Cab drivers and waiters, and a few others. And the proprietor of our boarding house was neat, but I'm not sure he qualifies as a native. He's an Englishman who's lived on the island for twenty years—a writer and painter who doesn't appear to be too successful. It's a quiet, lazy life. I can see how a person would lose his ambition in an idyllic spot like that.

SCENE 3. Being directly asked your opinion about a controversial topic

An informal backyard barbecue. You are with a group of friends, all of whom happen to be the parents of high school students. They are talking about college plans and the changes in dormitory living that have occurred in recent years, specifically co-ed dormitories and the sexual freedom of the contem-

porary college scene. *You have been listening quietly, but as usual you are not contributing anything to the discussion. You have a daughter entering college next year and have been giving considerable thought to this problem, but you're not absolutely sure what you think. Suddenly a member of the group turns to you and addresses you directly. You feel your heart sink and your mind go blank but tell yourself firmly that your opinion is just as worthwhile as theirs.*

SHE: What do *you* think about this, Joan? You're keeping very quiet.

YOU: I'm having a hard time deciding where I stand. It was certainly more reassuring for parents when colleges assumed a parental role—like they did when we were there. On the other hand, I suppose if a student is old enough to go away to college he should be able to make his own decisions about what to do.

SHE: But don't you worry about your daughter in a situation like that?

YOU: I do worry about it, and I'm not happy with the idea, but I can't see any way of avoiding the problem other than not sending her to college or telling her to live at home and commute to U.B. If I did that, she'd probably leave home anyway.

SCENE 4. Disagreeing with a majority opinion

The company cafeteria. You are having lunch with several co-workers on a spring day when people are beginning to make vacation plans. One member of the group is spending August on Nantucket; another is going to her parents' summer home in Nova Scotia. A third is planning a trip to France and has been busily mapping out her itinerary with a travel agent. She comments that she can't imagine how so many people go on group tours when you can do just as well financially with the new low air fares and at the same time can visit exactly the places you want to visit. The other two members of the group express their avid agreement. It just happens that you have recently signed up for a singles package tour to Spain. You are beginning to feel uncomfortable about being in the minority, but decide to get yourself together and voice your opinion.

> YOU: I don't agree with you at all. I think package tours are great, especially for inexperienced travelers who are traveling alone.
>
> ONE OF THEM: But don't you think it would be very confining to be with a group of other tourists?
>
> YOU: No, I know it isn't. I went on a package cruise last year—the travel agent suggested it, since I was traveling alone and the tour was for singles under thirty-five. There were a lot of other people around, but since I was with other single people, I could always find someone to talk to or go sightseeing with. I'd feel uncomfortable being completely alone.
>
> ONE OF THEM: After going on one package tour, would you actually go on another?
>
> YOU: Yes, I'm going on a package tour to Spain in September. There's no way I could possibly see as much on my own and I prefer to let somebody else make all the hotel arrangements and see that the baggage gets picked up. Maybe after I've had a chance to travel more I'll feel differently, but right now I think a tour is the best answer for me.

SCENE 5. Speaking up about what YOU would like to do

The living room of a small apartment. You and your date have stopped by to pick up the couple you are going out to dinner with, and the four of you are discussing where to go. The three of them are very fond of Mexican food, and it seems to you that whenever you go out together you end up eating at a Mexican restaurant. While you don't have anything against nachos and tacos, you're not in the mood for them tonight.

> ONE OF THEM: There's a new Mexican place in Westport that we haven't tried.
>
> ANOTHER: Have you heard anything about it?

FIRST ONE: Yes, Sally was there last weekend and says the food is terrific.

ANOTHER: I'm for that. It sounds like something we'd all enjoy.

YOU: Somehow I'm not in the mood for Mexican food tonight. I'm beginning to feel that when I go out with the three of you I ought to polish up my Spanish. How about trying that Mandarin place on the Post Road?

ONE OF THEM: What's wrong with Mexican food?

YOU: Not a thing. I like it—once in a while. But this is getting to be a habit.

ONE OF THEM: You never said you didn't like it.

YOU: I do like it! I just feel like going someplace different this time. And I usually haven't wanted to argue if everyone else wanted Mexican food. But I've heard the Mandarin Inn is exceptionally good. Some of their dishes are almost as hot as Mexican food.

GROUP: Let's give it a try.

How 10 to Approach Authorities and Celebrities

I would rank talking to authorities and celebrities third in my list of difficulties for shy people; first come those of the opposite sex, second come people in groups.

Authorities and celebrities rank third, I think because they don't present such a frequent or such an unavoidable problem. At the same time, if you are paralyzed with anxiety every time you have to say good morning to your boss or ask a professor a question after class, you are in for some pretty uncomfortable moments. One of my clients, a receptionist, felt herself blushing every time her boss walked into the room and she was faced with the prospect of making conversation with him (see Chapter 12). An accounting student reported that he could not ask his accounting professor to explain points he did not understand; he'd tried on a few occasions but felt so acutely conscious of his anxiety that he was unable to follow the explanation. When he entered my Shyness Clinic he was passing accounting only by having his uncle, an accountant, go over the work with him.

Another client, a Ph.D. candidate at a prestigious university, could handle social conversations with the professors in her department (many of whom had national and even international reputations) but was terrified at the thought of discussing her work with them. She feared they would ask questions she couldn't answer adequately, constantly envisioned herself saying "something stupid," and was devastated by the slightest criticism of her work.

Since she was working on her dissertation research when she consulted me, meetings with her advisor and other professors on her thesis committee were rather frequent. The resulting discomfort almost caused her to withdraw from the university before completing her degree.

Lawyers and doctors, including psychiatrists, are also imposing authority figures to most people, especially women. One particularly shy client informed me that for two years she had been seeing a psychiatrist who made her so nervous she couldn't talk to him and "just sat there" during her visits. When I asked why she had continued going, she replied, "I was afraid that if I stopped going, I'd get worse."

Numerous clients have reported being unable to insist that their physicians fully explain the details of forthcoming operations, ask for a second opinion, or even obtain adequate information about the condition of a hospitalized family member. While many doctors do treat their patients with respect and take the time to answer questions fully, unfortunately many other members of the medical profession treat patients in a condescending or patronizing manner.

I will never forget one encounter I had with a brash young physician who was taking care of my eighty-year-old father following his second heart attack. After several efforts

I managed to capture his attention for a brief conversation in the hospital hall. I explained that I was planning to return East to my family and my work on Sunday, and asked if he felt it was necessary for me to stay longer. He looked at me coldly and said "That depends entirely on your relationship with your father."

Angered by his implication that I didn't care for my father, I looked at him equally coldly and replied "I consider that a very insulting remark." After that, we had no further difficulties—in fact, he became surprisingly pleasant.

Many women have complained to me about their physician's habit of calling them by their first names, while he is Dr. So-and-So to them. Others feel that the doctor is only trying to be friendly or put them at ease; still others feel that he has "earned" this privilege through his long years of preparation for his career.

If talking with such everyday types of authority figures as professors, doctors, and lawyers is so difficult for shy people, what about encounters with celebrities?

Needless to say, such encounters are likely to make anxieties soar even higher. I remember as a fledgling feature writer for the college newspaper being assigned to interview Katherine Anne Porter when she came to Wellesley as a visiting lecturer. The interview had been scheduled for the afternoon preceding her lecture. When the famous lady called to say she had come down with a case of laryngitis and would have to save all of her voice for the lecture, I couldn't decide which emotion was stronger: my disappointment at missing out on my big chance or my relief at not having to interview such a celebrity.

Much later, writing feature articles for the Bridgeport *Post*, I had the opportunity to interview numerous celebrities, including Pauline Trigère, Vance Packard, and James Daugherty. But in some ways it is the terror of anticipating that first interview, though it never materialized, which I remember most clearly.

In her book, *How to Talk with Practically Anybody about Practically Anything*, Barbara Walters describes a fruitful interview with Aristotle Onassis, which she got off the ground with the remark "Tell me, Mr. Onassis, you're so successful—not just in shipping and airlines, but in other industries too—I wonder, how did you begin? What was your very first job?" She contrasts this experience with one much earlier in her career, when on being introduced to Truman Capote at a party, she could come up with nothing but "How do you do, Mr. Capote?" Though she'd recently read *In Cold Blood* and wanted to talk with him about it, she was overcome with shyness and feared Capote would be tired of people talking to him about his books.

Few of us will ever match Barbara Walters in experience or skill in talking with celebrities, but many of her suggestions can be utilized in situations more likely to occur in everyday life. And it isn't actually that rare to encounter a well-known person. One of my clients recently reported that she recognized Joan Walsh Anglund, the writer and illustrator of children's books, while purchasing art supplies. "You must be getting through to me," she declared when I next saw her. "I didn't just walk away but told her how much I admired her work. She was perfectly charming and we had a lovely conversation."

Another client, a young man temporarily working as a caddy, recognized sportscaster Jim McKay on the golf course one morning. His impulse was to go up and express his enjoyment of the programs he had seen, but he made the mistake of discussing his idea with the other caddies and letting himself be dissuaded by their disparaging remarks.

His original impulse was a good one. As Barbara Walters points out, "You can safely begin a conversation with any famous person—or with anyone at all, for that matter—by indulging your natural impulse to express admiration." Don't mention a specific work to a writer or playwright unless you're certain your reference is correct, but don't hesitate to make a more general comment.

Of course you shouldn't impose on a celebrity who is eating dinner in a restaurant, or otherwise infringe on privacy. Dick Cavett, having achieved the fame he wanted so desperately earlier in his career, now complains that he can no longer go out without someone saying " 'Excuse me, I know I'm bothering you.' And I want to say, 'Yes, right so far.' "

Good taste is an important consideration in deciding when or how to approach a celebrity. Ask human-interest questions but avoid the overly personal. If you are sincerely interested in the other person and manage to get that interest across, your celebrity will be likely to respond in the same way.

If you are going to be attending a social event where a well-known person will be the guest of honor, it is a good idea to do a little library research and find out something about the person ahead of time. Then you can ask about hobbies or special interests and say something about related interests of your own if the occasion presents itself.

Don't make the mistake of trying to discuss technical details of an occupation you know nothing about. As noted, Barbara Walters suggests good questions to ask a successful person: "How did you get started? What was your very first job?" Another is "How do you manage to fit everything into such a busy schedule?" If you want to make a controversial statement, in a social context it is frequently best to say, "I've heard it said that . . ." or "I know some people feel that . . . what is your reaction to that point of view?"

Probably the most important point to remember is that celebrities are people, too.

ACT I. ASK THE PROFESSOR

SCENE 1. Asking the professor a question after class

A college class in introductory psychology. Most of the students have left the room, but a few stragglers are still collecting notebooks and papers. You approach the professor to ask for an explanation about something you did not understand.

YOU: Professor Allen, you referred several times in today's lecture to the "null hypothesis." This isn't a term I'm familiar with. Could you please explain it?

PROFESSOR: In conducting any statistical test or experiment—comparing the scores of two different populations, for example—the null hypothesis is that there is actually no difference between the two groups. If the statistical test indicates that there *is* a difference, too large to have occurred by chance, the null hypothesis is rejected and we assume that the two groups are significantly different.

YOU: Thank you. I think I understand it now.

SCENE 2. Discussing a grade with a professor

A professor's office. You have stopped by to discuss your midterm grade. According to a note you received from the dean, you are getting a D in English. You were expecting a B.

YOU: Professor Jones, I'm Mike Harrington. I'm in your English 210 class. I've just received a note from the dean saying my midterm grade is a D.

PROFESSOR: And?

YOU: I think this must be a mistake. I had a B minus on the paper you assigned, and a B on the midterm, so I don't understand how I could be getting a D.

PROFESSOR: I double-checked all these grades before submitting them to the registrar.

YOU: But a mistake must have occurred somehow. This just couldn't possibly be correct. Could you check your records again?

PROFESSOR: Well, I suppose anything is possible. Just let me find my files here. . . . Yes, you are right. I see here that you should have received a B. Don't worry about it.

YOU: Will you put through a correction?

PROFESSOR: This is only a midterm grade. It doesn't go on your permanent record anyway, so that won't be necessary.

YOU: In my case it is necessary. My scholarship won't be renewed for next year if I have this D on my record.

PROFESSOR: All right, then, I will send in a correction to the dean.

YOU: Thank you.

SCENE 3. Asking a professor to be your advisor

A professor's office. You have arrived for an appointment in which you plan to tell the professor you plan to major in economics and to ask him to be your advisor. You have had two classes with this professor, but do not know him personally, and are feeling nervous about making this request.

YOU: Dr. Sheffield, I'm Debbie O'Connor. I'm declaring economics as my major and would like to have you as my advisor.

HE: I'll be glad to serve in that capacity.

YOU: Thank you very much.

HE: When you are ready to preregister for fall courses, please set up another appointment with me first. I'd like to look over your entire program with you. I feel you should have at least one course in natural science and one in the humanities even though the college doesn't have these as general requirements.

YOU: That sounds like a good idea to me.

HE: Since you're going to be an economics major, you're invited to the department party Wednesday night. It starts at nine in the multipurpose room.

YOU: Fine, I'll be there.

SCENE 4. Discussing a professor's criticism of the project on which you plan to do your thesis

A professor's office. You have completed more than half the research for your senior thesis project and were under the impression that your plans had been formally approved. Now the professor has notified you that your proposal is still lacking formal approval and that he considers it very limited in scope. You are hoping to straighten out the situation as quickly as possible so you can continue with your data collection. You are afraid of bursting into tears during the interview.

YOU: Professor Goldberg, I'd like to talk to you about my thesis project. I was surprised to receive your note this week, because I thought everything had been squared away.

PROFESSOR: You must have overlooked the fact that certain procedures have to be followed in this university. Your committee members must send in formal letters of approval.

YOU: Is it going to be a problem getting their approval now that I am halfway into my data collection?

PROFESSOR: Probably not an insurmountable problem.

YOU: I'll take care of that right away. But something else is bothering me. I had the impression from your note that you had decided my project wasn't worth doing.

PROFESSOR: I didn't say that exactly. I said I felt it was very limited in scope.

YOU: It was my intention to do an in-depth study of a relatively small sample, rather than a superficial analysis of a larger number of cases.

PROFESSOR: Yes, well, we'll have to see what you turn up. It may work out all right.

YOU: But Professor Goldberg, you are my major advisor!

I've been discussing this with you all along. Do I have
your approval of this project?

PROFESSOR: Yes, I think it will be all right.

YOU: May I please have a formal letter of approval for
submission to the dean?

PROFESSOR: Yes, you can pick it up tomorrow.

YOU: Thank you.

ACT II. MEDICAL MATTERS

SCENE 1. Asking a doctor for a fuller explanation

*Your physician just informed you that you have a duodenal
ulcer. You have always considered ulcers a serious condition
and are quite alarmed at this news.*

DOCTOR: Everything is going to be all right, Mary. Just
follow my instructions carefully and you'll have
nothing to worry about.

YOU: I don't understand what causes ulcers, Dr. Atkins.
Could you please explain?

DOCTOR: No need for you to trouble yourself with these
details, Mary. Tell me, did anything upsetting happen in your life around the time you first noticed
these symptoms?

YOU: Bob and I started talking about getting a divorce.
We haven't gone through with it, but things aren't
getting any better either. Are you suggesting this
ulcer is a psychosomatic problem?

DOCTOR: Ulcers usually are.

YOU: But these are *physical* symptoms I'm having. Do you
mean I'm just imagining them?

DOCTOR: Not at all. The symptoms are very real.

YOU: I'm afraid I'm still not clear about this. Are you
saying that emotional factors actually caused a physical illness?

DOCTOR: Yes, that is often the case. Most ulcer patients
have a built-in physiological susceptibility to ulcers,

which is probably hereditary. Under stressful emotional conditions, especially of a prolonged nature, people with this physiological tendency are likely to develop ulcers. .

YOU: Thank you for explaining. I think I understand. Where do we go from here?

SCENE 2. Complaining to a doctor about how long you were kept waiting

A doctor's office. Your doctor is a friendly young man whom you like very much, except for one problem: every time you go to his office you spend more than an hour waiting. Today it is bothering you particularly because you have waited even longer than usual and now are likely to be late for your next appointment.

DOCTOR: Hello, Mrs. Smith. Sorry to keep you waiting. I hope it hasn't inconvenienced you.

YOU: As a matter of fact, it has. I'm going to be late for a five-o'clock appointment.

DOCTOR: I'm sorry. There are always so many unexpected things that come up in a doctor's office.

YOU: I could easily understand and accept that if it happened once or twice, Dr. Atkins, but it happens every single time I come. I'm very busy myself and it is upsetting to waste so much time this way. I'm beginning to think you go in for deliberate overbooking—and personally I don't think that's any way to run an airline!

DOCTOR: I really *am* sorry. Next time, please request the earliest appointment, at nine A.M. That way you shouldn't have to wait.

YOU: Thank you. That's a good idea.

SCENE 3. Telling a doctor you prefer to be called "Mrs. Smith"

A doctor's office. Your doctor, a man of about your own age or possibly a few years younger, comes to the reception room and smiles at you in a friendly way.

DOCTOR: Come in, Mary! It's nice to see you.
YOU: Hello, Dr. Atkins.
DOCTOR: How have you been feeling, Mary?
YOU: I'm feeling fine, but I thought it was time for a check-up. There's something I'd like to talk to you about now that I'm here, though.
DOCTOR: Of course, Mary. What is it?
YOU: That's what it is. It's a little difficult for me to say this, Dr. Atkins, but it makes me feel uncomfortable for you to call me "Mary" when I call you "Dr. Atkins." I'd be happier if you called me "Mrs. Smith."
DOCTOR: I'm sorry. I can understand how you feel, and I'm glad you mentioned it. I'll try to change over to "Mrs. Smith," but forgive me if I slip back to my old ways once in a while. But wait—I have a different idea—why don't you call me Peter?
YOU: That's nice of you. But calling you Peter would probably be even harder for me than calling me Mrs. Smith would be for you!

ACT III. STARS ABOVE

SCENE 1. Asking a question (one-to-one) of a celebrity after a lecture

A school auditorium. You have attended a lecture given by Governor Jenny Jones and stay afterward to discuss a particular question with her.

YOU: Governor Jones, I enjoyed your lecture very much and wanted to ask you what advice you would give a young woman hoping to have a career in politics.
SHE: Get involved. Do anything you can at the local level by

140   OVERCOMING SHYNESS

volunteering to work in campaigns and help out at headquarters.

YOU: Do you think an aspiring politician should plan to get a law degree?

SHE: It's a help. Obviously not all politicians are lawyers, but a big proportion of them are.

YOU: Why do you think there are still so few women in politics?

SHE: I don't think enough women have had the interest or made the effort. It's a tough business—for men *or* women. If you're determined enough, your determination will pay off.

YOU: I hope so. Thank you, Governor Jones.

SCENE 2. Conversing with a celebrity at a reception in his or her honor

You are attending a tea given in honor of Amanda Crispie, a well-known and very successful mystery writer. You have long been an enthusiastic fan of her work. To your surprise, Mrs. Crispie is a rather conventional-looking middle-aged woman. But you feel overawed by her accomplishments and are somewhat taken aback to find yourself standing next to her. Momentarily you glance around hoping for rescue; then you decide to be as brave as you can about this.

YOU: Mrs. Crispie, I think I've read every single one of your books, and some of them several times. I'd like to thank you for all the hours of pleasure you've given me.

SHE: That's a very nice thing to say, and one any writer would be pleased to hear. Thank you.

YOU: Every time I find myself at a paperback book counter, I check the titles again to see if there's one of yours I've missed. But there never is! I've often wondered how you come up with so much accurate background information.

SHE: Oh, an acute observer picks up new pieces of useful information every day. But I'd say my experience as a nurse gave me firsthand knowledge of medical matters

How to Approach Authorities and Celebrities   **141**

that has been very valuable, and my travels with my husband have made me familiar with many exotic locales I could never have depicted otherwise.

SCENE 3. Calling a celebrity (or a very busy professional person) to ask for information

You are a high school biology teacher. Since news of a British "test-tube" baby made international news, some of your advanced placement students have been asking you questions you can't answer. A physician doing related research happens to live in your city.

> YOU: Dr. Terman, my name is Evelyn Anderson. I teach biology and advanced placement biology at Central High School. Since the British test-tube baby was born, my advanced placement students, most of whom hope to be doctors, are asking me all sorts of questions I can't answer. I'm calling you with the hope that you can tell me something about the procedure. It's so new that I have no idea where else to turn for information.
>
> DOCTOR: I'll be glad to do what I can to help. The term *test-tube baby* has been unfortunate. There is no baby in the test tube—just a few cells.
>
> YOU: I know the procedure is for women who have no other hope of becoming pregnant, but exactly what is their medical problem?
>
> DOCTOR: If the fallopian tubes are blocked and surgery cannot correct the problem, the test-tube procedure might be appropriate. At present, the U.S. government is not funding research in this field, which means that candidates for the procedure will have to go out of the country.
>
> YOU: What is your opinion of the ethical issues involved?
>
> DOCTOR: It does pose some difficult problems, but in my opinion this is reasonable procedure for women who can't conceive due to blocked fallopian tubes. Each

case would have to be considered individually by the woman, her husband, and her physician.

YOU: Thank you very much, Dr. Terman.

SCENE 4. Telephoning a celebrity to arrange a speech for an organization you belong to

This assumes you have been able to penetrate the barrier of secretaries, assistants, and so on that usually surrounds a celebrity. This assumption may be unreasonable.

YOU: Dr. Shinner, this is Mona Delrio. I'm the program chairman for the Valley Psychological Association. We would like very much to have you speak at one of our spring meetings. We meet on the third Wednesday of the month and usually have a business meeting at seven-thirty followed by a lecture at eight-thirty. Either March or April would be fine with us.

HE: Let's see, I'll have to check my calendar. I will be out of the country the third week of March, but as far as I can see here, I could make it in April.

YOU: We haven't discussed fees. I'm sure you usually charge a very high price, but we have a very small budget. Is there any way we can work out something satisfactory?

HE: I either charge a very high price or nothing at all. In your case the fee will be nothing at all.

YOU: Dr. Shinner, we appreciate this very much. I'll schedule you definitely for April nineteenth, then. And if you could send me some biographical information and a glossy photograph, I can take care of the newspaper publicity. My address is seventy-five Old Rock Lane.

HE: I'll get it off to you soon.

YOU: Thank you. I'll be looking forward to meeting you.

How to Make 11 Troublesome Phone Calls

Most shy people find it difficult to make certain telephone calls—asking for a date, for example, or calling to set up a job interview.

Other kinds of phone calls, even relatively routine ones, produce varying amounts of anxiety for different shy people. Some such calls involve taking assertive action, like making necessary complaints or demands. Others concern such everyday matters as making appointments, asking for information, replying to advertisements, leaving a message for someone to call you back, or returning a call received when you were out.

This chapter will concentrate on the everyday kind of phone call.

One teenager in a high school Shyness Clinic wanted to practice calling a dentist for an appointment, something she had never done because her mother always did it for her. Some routine calls to doctors and other professionals are surprisingly difficult to make, even for adults. Geri wanted to discuss a problem with her gynecologist. She didn't think a visit was necessary, but didn't want to explain her problem to the nurse. And as we all know, doctors' nurses and receptionists belong to a particularly assertive group of people. Geri practiced insisting on speaking to the doctor while politely declining to discuss the problem with the nurse. Because she felt so much anxiety about it I had her make the call from my office, and it turned out to be much less difficult than she had anticipated.

One call that is troublesome for almost anyone is the initial phone call to a mental health professional. This call is emotionally charged, since much conflict and soul-searching have usually preceded it. It may be somewhat easier if you have been personally referred by a physician or friend, but this isn't necessarily true.

It is perfectly acceptable to ask questions—to ascertain whether the person is experienced or knowledgeable about your particular problem, what the fee is, and whether the therapy is covered by your insurance policy. It is all right to ask about the person's credentials, and as I have said elsewhere I recommend that you go only to a person who is a fully qualified member of one of the three recognized mental health professions—psychiatry (M.D.), psychology (Ph.D.), or social work (M.S.W.)—unless you know through unquestionable recommendations that a particular individual's personal qualifications outweigh his or her lack of academic credentials.

Many people are not only shy about making the initial call, but they are shy about leaving their name and number with an answering service. I know that some potential clients have never reached me because they were too shy or embarrassed to leave their name, or didn't want another family member to receive the return call. I think answering machines are even more intimidating to the shy person than a live voice at the other end, and do not use one for that reason.

Calling to arrange for lessons or get information about courses being offered can also be difficult for some people. Beverly wanted to start taking golf lessons at the country club to which she belonged, but had trouble getting herself to call the pro to set up the first lesson. Another wanted to join the painting class taught by a well-known artist but couldn't get herself to make the call to find out about it.

Jane, a college girl in another clinic, had to call the dean at her school to make arrangements about transferring credit from the school where she was taking a summer course. She was so nervous about making the call that she had put it off for a week when she finally brought it up in a group session. After practicing several times in the group, Jane was able to make the call. She reported that it wasn't easy, and that she could "almost feel her voice shaking," but that she had a real feeling of accomplishment for having done it. The next week she had to make another call to the same dean and felt considerably more relaxed the second time around.

The rules for routine phone calls are: First, introduce yourself by name and tell the voice at the other end why you are calling and, second, ask any necessary questions. If you think you may forget your questions, write them down beforehand.

ACT I. MORE MEDICAL MATTERS

SCENE 1. Calling to make a routine appointment with a new doctor

VOICE: Dr. Smith's office.
YOU: I'd like to make an appointment to see Dr. Smith.
VOICE: Name, please.
YOU: Mrs. Ginger Jones.
VOICE: Have you been here before?
YOU: No.
VOICE: Can you tell me what the problem is?
YOU: Nothing special. I just need a routine checkup.
VOICE: Dr. Smith can see you at ten on Thursday.
YOU: I'm sorry, that won't be convenient. The best time for me is in the afternoon, any day but Wednesday.
VOICE: All right, how about next Friday at two?
YOU: Fine, I'll be there.

SCENE 2. Calling to speak personally to a doctor

VOICE: Dr. Smith's office.
YOU: This is Janet Curtis. I'd like to speak with Dr. Smith, please.
VOICE: Dr. Smith is busy right now. What is this concerning?
YOU: It's something I prefer to discuss personally with Dr. Smith.
VOICE: He's not free now.
YOU: Would you please have him call me when he's free?
VOICE: I'll give him the message. What's your number?
YOU: 838-9213.

SCENE 3. Calling to make an appointment with a therapist

VOICE: Hello, this is Dr. Jones.
YOU: Dr. Jones, my name is Gwendolyn Spence. I was referred to you by Dr. Peter Smith.
VOICE: Yes, what can I do for you?
YOU: I have a problem with insomnia. Dr. Smith seems to think the problem is psychological.
VOICE: Have you had any psychiatric treatment before?
YOU: No, never. What is your fee, Dr. Jones?
VOICE: Fifty dollars per session.
YOU: Do you have much success in treating insomnia?

How to Make Troublesome Phone Calls   147

VOICE: With most patients I do. Of course I can't guarantee
        anything.
  YOU: I understand that. I'd like to make an appointment.
        Do you have evening hours?
VOICE: Yes. I could see you Thursday evening at six.
  YOU: Thank you. I'll be there.

Act II. Phony Business

Scene 1. Leaving your name and number with an answering machine

RECORDED VOICE: At the sound of the tone, please
        leave your name and number, and I will return your
        call as soon as possible.
  YOU: This is Mary Ellen Osgood, 949-6222. Please call
        me between six and nine this evening.

Scene 2. Returning a call received when you were out

VOICE: Dr. Smith's office.
  YOU: This is Janet Curtis, returning your call.
VOICE: Thank you for calling back. We just called to remind
        you of your appointment tomorrow at four.
  YOU: Yes, I haven't forgotten. I'll be there.

Scene 3. Calling for information about a course advertised in the newspaper

VOICE: Hello.
  YOU: Hello. My name is Gladys Winkler. I'm calling about
        the ceramics class advertised in the paper. Could you
        tell me a little more about it, please?
VOICE: I'll be glad to. What would you like to know?
  YOU: What is the fee?
VOICE: Fifty dollars for five sessions.
  YOU: What time do the classes meet?
VOICE: I have one on Tuesdays from seven to nine P.M. and

one on Thursdays from nine to eleven A.M. Both groups start next week.

YOU: How many people will be in the class?

VOICE: Each group is limited to eight.

YOU: I'd like to join the morning class.

VOICE: Fine. Can you drop your check in the mail to me, or bring it by?

YOU: I'll bring it over this afternoon if you'll give me directions to your place.

Overcoming 12 Shyness on the Job

Excessive shyness on the job can be more than a handicap. It can be a total disaster.

It can stand in your way of promotions, hamper you in making the business contacts you need for success, or keep you from getting hired in the first place. It can even stop you from making the initial phone call you need to make to set up an appointment for a job interview. And success in the corporate world is highly dependent on the ability to communicate effectively.

If you are a professional in private practice, shyness can keep you from relating comfortably to your patients or clients. A shy doctor or lawyer isn't able to put shy clients at ease, and is more likely to remain in a confining salaried position than to opt for more lucrative independent practice.

Whether you are a clerk at the drugstore or an interior

decorator dealing with wealthy homeowners, shyness will be a handicap in any business situation that involves meeting the public.

It's obvious that certain career fields would be unsuitable for shy people. Sales is the one that comes to mind most quickly, yet I have had several real estate agents in assertive training groups. One was so uncomfortable speaking up in a group that she did not return after the first session. Understandably, she was not doing well in the competitive field of real estate.

Sometimes shy people actually go into sales fields because they think it will help them overcome their problem, and sometimes it does. In other cases they remain miserable or leave the field to avoid their misery. Even in careers where the image of the typical worker is that of a quiet, reserved person, a certain amount of interpersonal contact is a daily necessity. Take library work, for example. A librarian talks to people all day answering reference questions, helping readers find books, and so forth.

After devoting considerable thought to the topic, I have been unable to think of a single occupation where excessive shyness would not be a drawback. Possibly it wouldn't matter much for a lighthouse keeper or a forester, or someone else working in a reclusive situation where there is literally no contact with others. I suspect that most people who end up in such occupations do so *because* they are excessively shy and want to avoid contact with others.

The scientist working away in his or her laboratory may not be much troubled because of shyness most of the time, but how will he or she manage when findings have to be discussed with the head of the laboratory or the department chairman, or a research paper has to be presented at a scholarly meeting? The struggling artist or poet may avoid the public by hiding away in a garret, but what happens when he or she becomes successful and is the guest of honor at a cocktail party, is invited to appear on the Johnny Carson show, or must make arrangements for an exhibition at a gallery? One best-selling author was caught unprepared by his overnight success and had to adjust quickly to frequent television appearances.

In most work situations the ability to handle business communications, not making small talk, is most important. If you can't handle yourself in a job interview, you won't get the job. If you can't communicate with your boss or your client, you won't keep the job or get promotions, and if you can't communicate with your subordinates, you may not be able to keep *them.* The ability to converse socially with business colleagues at conventions or on the golf course is also essential in some career fields, notably sales.

Some kinds of communication that are effective and desirable in social situations and interpersonal relationships are not appropriate on the job—primarily talking about feelings. Temperamental displays have no place in the office, and in most cases you would be well-advised to express personal feelings, *when necessary,* in as straightforward and businesslike a way as possible.

It goes without saying that being able to communicate effectively on the job, make small talk at parties, or come across assertively at business conferences is not going to win you a promotion if you don't handle other aspects of the job successfully. As one market-research executive told me recently, "The bottom line is getting the job done."

Almost everyone, shy or not shy, is apprehensive about looking for a job. This is completely understandable, because one doesn't look for a job that often. In this situation you are putting yourself, not a product or a service, on the line, and rejection at any point in the process can therefore be devastating. To maximize your chances of finding the job that is right for you, and to minimize the anxieties you are almost certain to be feeling, it is important to plan your campaign carefully—regardless of the level of employment you are seeking.

As a first step in planning your job-hunting campaign, read two books: Carl Boll's *Executive Jobs Unlimited* (available in both hardcover and paperback) and R. J. Jameson's *Professional Job Changing System* (available from Performance Dynamics, Verona, N.J., or through any bookstore). Don't rely on one of these books alone; they provide different approaches. Both are good, but you may be more comfortable with one than the other or may wish to integrate suggestions from both. To acquire further information and clarify the ideas you have already obtained, you may also find it helpful to read additional books on job-seeking techniques; every library has several.

Having thoughtfully completed this reading, you are now in a position to map out your strategy in detail. At this point it would be a good idea to order some conservative printed (not engraved) stationery (choose a good rag bond) so it will be available when you need it. The importance of effective correspondence throughout a job-seeking campaign cannot be overemphasized.

Next, use your local library as a resource to help you develop a list of potential employers who could provide the opportunity you are looking for. Standard business and financial directories, annual reports, local business directories, and newspaper and magazine articles (check the *Reader's Guide to Periodical Literature*) should give you most of the information you need. If you are uncertain as to how to proceed, ask your librarian for assistance. Use a 4-by-6 index card to record information about each firm that interests you.

Once you have identified prospective employers, check through your cards carefully with the idea of finding a personal contact to a key individual in the firm. Most positions are obtained through personal contact. If you give sufficient thought to this important phase of your job search, you will be surprised at how many contacts you can develop.

Concurrently, do not neglect the possibilities offered by advertisements in national and local newspapers and business publications. You should be reading and answering ads daily as a regular part of your job campaign. Don't be surprised if you receive few replies to answers to blind ads—but you never know when your effort will be rewarded.

Now let's get back to the job interview, or even one step before it: calling for an appointment or visiting an employment agency. If you are calling in response to a newspaper advertisement, the task should not be overly difficult. You call and identify yourself clearly, and say that you would like to arrange an interview for the position advertised in the paper. You may be asked at this time about your prior experience, and you should have an answer prepared. I have had several women in assertive training groups who felt thoroughly intimidated by such a phone call, usually because they had not held a job for many years. After several demonstrations and rehearsals, they made the initial call from the group session. They all found that the first one was the hardest—and they were able to go on to arrange subsequent interviews with more self-confidence. (When attempting to set up several interviews, always make the call for the least desirable position first. You'll feel less anxiety about the conversation and will gain practice for the more important calls you'll make later.)

You may be calling about a job that a friend, acquaintance, or an employment agent told you about, in which case the best introduction is usually "My name is Betty Smith.

Joe Flanders suggested I call you about the job you have open. I'd like to make an appointment to talk with you about it."

Visiting an employment agency, like making an initial call in response to an ad, may be a problem for shy people. One shy young man told me he had walked by six employment agencies before getting up the nerve to go in. He finally pushed himself to do it by promising himself a new pair of golf shoes—a reward he really wanted. Subsequent agencies were much less threatening after that first experience.

Arranging an interview is a little more complicated if you are not applying for a specific job but are looking for information about a field or company. If you are honestly not looking for a job, you may stand a better chance of getting an interview if you make that clear in your initial phone call.

John Crystal, probably the country's leading career consultant, recommends that you find ways of arranging coincidental, informal meetings with "Prime Targets" (key people who do the hiring)—at church, at the golf club, or on the tennis court. Crystal claims that "the last place to look for a job—a really good, interesting job—is an employment agency or personnel office of a company." My own experience and that of my clients suggest that he is right.

Most people, especially shy ones, wouldn't be as adept at Crystal's elaborate battle-plan approach as John Crystal himself. An ex-U.S. spy behind enemy lines during World War II, he developed his unconventional procedures when a more traditional approach failed to land him a job after the war. Crystal recommends the development of a five- to ten-year objective through extensive personal exploration and consideration of life experiences, followed by an equally extensive investigation through reading and personal interviews, making the most of a "contacts list" to obtain introduction to the Prime Targets who have been identified.

Those who are interested in the Crystal approach can obtain a schedule of free introductory lectures, one-day workshops ($60), and full fifty-hour courses ($500 to $635) from the John C. Crystal Center Inc., 894 Plaindome Road, Manhasset, N.Y. 11030; telephone 516–627–8802. Many other organizations also offer helpful career planning seminars and workshops.

Once you have reached the interview stage of your campaign, it is vitally important to do your homework before you arrive. This is expected at the management level and is a plus at any level. Find out all you can about the company and about the person who is interviewing you, and be prepared to ask questions that will clearly reveal your interest and knowledge. In addition, try to imagine all of the questions you are likely to be asked and come up with reasonable answers to them. Don't try to memorize your lines, but do have a general idea of how to handle potentially difficult queries. One third-year law student, at the point of scheduling interviews with potential law firms, discovered she was most afraid of being asked what she had been doing for the seven years between college and law school. (She had produced and raised a son.) She considered various ways of handling this question and decided she would be most comfortable with the truth: "I was raising my son."

Another woman, the mother of three children, who was returning to a copywriting job after a ten-year hiatus, dreaded being asked how she planned to handle the baby-sitting problems she would encounter, especially if children were sick. She decided to counter with "I have already made satisfactory arrangements—otherwise I wouldn't be returning to work." Unmarried women are frequently asked how marriage will affect their career plans, and young married women are asked if they plan to have children. I remember being asked this myself when, at twenty-three, I was interviewed for a copywriting job at *Parade*. I replied firmly that I didn't plan to have any children for a long time. I got the job and became pregnant a few months later (but it was true that I hadn't planned to).

These days, employers may feel somewhat less free to ask personal questions of women than they did twenty-five years ago, but I think this still happens frequently. If you find yourself in such a situation, you are legally within your rights if you refuse to answer the question or say that you consider it irrelevant—but from a practical point of view, that attitude will not help you get the job. I advise clients to answer a direct personal question pleasantly, briefly, and firmly, and to discourage this line of questioning without being openly rude. Never volunteer personal information in an interview, and if asked directly say only as much as is necessary.

Many people, men as well as women, seem to be under the impression that a certain amount of personal information belongs on a résumé. I was suffering under this misapprehension myself until a New York career counselor, with whom I worked briefly as co-leader of a group counseling program, pointed out that my résumé didn't need to state that I was divorced and the mother of four children. I realized that he was absolutely correct, and immediately deleted this information from my résumé.

In general I don't advise using the traditional résumé at all any more, except in settings such as the academic marketplace, where a well-written *curriculum vita* is an absolute must. In most other cases, if a personal entrée is not available, a "selling letter" is much more appropriate initially, and the best model for such a letter can be found in Carl Boll's *Executive Jobs Unlimited*—even if you are not an executive but are looking for your first job after graduating from architectural school, or are hoping to be hired as a camp counselor. You may nevertheless be asked for a formal resumé—so prepare one in advance.

Whether you are using a résumé or a selling letter as a preliminary way of locating job possibilities, omit all personal information such as age, marital status, and number of children. If your age is going to be a drawback, omit dates after educational degrees and early work experience unless it is clearly pertinent. It goes without saying that there are exceptions to everything. If I were applying for a job as a psychologist in a college counseling center, I would mention the fact that I have four college-age children, since this information would be an asset.

When you are actually in an interview situation, you must try to sell yourself—not an easy task for anyone, but especially difficult for a shy person If you have prepared your questions and answers in advance, things will go more smoothly. You should tell the interviewer just why you would like to work there—even if you are not asked. Don't talk too much, but be sure not to answer questions with a yes or no and meekly wait to be asked another question.

Try to convey an aura of competence without arrogance, and don't downplay your abilities and experience. A woman in an assertive training group, a skilled writer who had published many feature articles in local publications and even in *The New York Times*, reported applying for an assistant editorship on a weekly newspaper. Asked if she had had experience as a newspaper staff writer, she replied "Yes—but it was a long time ago." And when the editor inquired if she had any knowledge of layout work, she said "I used to know how, but I've forgotten everything I knew." She did not get the job. Although she had a great deal to offer, she put her worst foot forward and portrayed herself in the poorest possible way. (Those without recent work experience might consider a temporary or part-time position to achieve more viability in the marketplace.)

It is important to maintain good eye contact during an interview (but avoid the constant stare) and to avoid fiddling with your hands. I have had to caution nervous women clients to make a conscious effort to keep their hands still during an interview. If you absolutely must have *something* to hold onto, a pencil or pen is probably best. When my Shyness Clinic was being filmed by the *Today* show, I had a clipboard and pen in my hand. Jane Pauley asked me if I actually used them or if I just needed something to hold onto—adding that she herself held a pen for security reasons!

Whatever you do, no matter how nervous you feel, do not smoke during the interview, even if the interviewer is smoking and offers you a cigarette.

Some interviewers make a deliberate effort to put you on the defensive at the beginning of the interview. They are interested in seeing how you handle stress. I remember one particularly unpleasant experience when I was being interviewed for a position as unit chief of a proposed behavior therapy unit at New York Hospital's Westchester division. The interviewer began by inquiring whether I was aware of an especially unfortunate typographical error in one of the articles I had submitted prior to the interview.

I had to admit that I wasn't aware of it, and he hastened to point it out. It was embarrassing, and about all I could say was "That certainly was an unfortunate mistake. Thank you for calling it to my attention. And now that we've taken care of that, why don't we get on to more important matters?" I didn't get the job—in fact, no one did, since the proposed unit never materialized—but I felt relatively satisfied with the way I had handled a very awkward situation. (When confronted with a stress interview, which is fortunately becoming less frequent, remember that the worst that can happen is a "no" or a temporary embarrassment. If the situation becomes unbearable, you can always get up, say you have changed your mind and are not interested in the position, and leave.)

Immediately following an interview, sit down in a coffee shop or in your car with an 8½-by-11 pad and list major aspects of the interview in sequence, no more than two to a page. Later, go back and fill in minor points and review strengths and weaknesses in your handling of the discussion. Don't block out what happened, as many do, but use this experience to make the next one more effective.

After an important interview, it is a very good idea to write a brief note thanking the person for his time and advice, and restating your interest in the position if it was an actual job interview. I have routinely done this myself and always advise my clients to do so. It goes without saying that your note must be typed.

You've Got the Job

Once you are actually hired, how big a problem is shyness likely to be?

Being sociable on the job—making casual conversation with your boss or co-workers—is one possible source of difficulty. For suggestions on handling this problem, see Chapters 6 and 9. Bear in mind that socializing on the job can be overdone. Don't conduct personal conversations during working hours and avoid office gossip at all times.

Work-oriented communication problems include asking co-workers for necessary information and giving directions to those working under you. If you need to know something or don't understand something you have been told, speak up. Often people are so afraid of sounding "stupid" that they avoid asking for necessary information and end up wasting a lot of time.

If you're shy and are suddenly thrust into a position that requires dealing with the public at other than a routine level, you are likely to feel quite ill at ease initially. One thing that will help is observing how experienced people in similar positions act. Exactly what do they say and do? It is all right to copy their exact words for a while. "Good morning, may I help you?" or "What can I do for you?" are reasonable openings in most situations. But look around you and listen. You'll be surprised at how much this will help.

Asking for a raise is a topic that frequently comes up in assertive training groups. Many people, especially women, are underpaid solely because they don't speak up and ask for a raise, and some employers are quick to take advantage of their reluctance. I've had women clients who insisted one "shouldn't have to ask" for a raise. The fact is that you do. And when asking for a raise, women often ask for too little, just as they frequently ask for too low a salary in the first place. Since money usually involves negotiating, always ask for somewhat more than you actually expect to get. Then you can compromise without feeling cheated. But your original request should not be ridiculously out of line, either. Try to appraise your market value realistically before naming an initial salary or asking for a raise. And then ask for a little bit more.

According to a recent study of *Fortune* 500 companies, reluctance to give instructions to secretaries and other subordinates is one of the major difficulties encountered by women on management levels. I have seen this numerous times in my own practice. One young woman, an office manager, would type letters herself rather than ask a secretary to do them over. A very shy publicity director employed by a large firm did everything she could to avoid asking secretaries to do anything for her. After several desensitization and rehearsal sessions she became much more comfortable with this aspect of her job.

Difficulties in giving instructions to subordinates are, of course, not limited to women. A fifty-year-old dentist with an established practice could not complain directly to one of his assistants that her X-rays had fingerprints on them; his way of handling the situation was to call a meeting of all his assistants, point out how important it was for X-rays to be free of fingerprints, and hope the guilty person would take the hint!

At management levels, the two additional communication issues most likely to present problems are, first, getting your point across in business meetings, both formal and informal, and second, making presentations.

Leon, an engineer with a major oil company, came to me for help because he experienced severe anxiety symptoms in business conferences and was so uncomfortable making sales presentations that he avoided them whenever possible, though he knew this behavior was preventing his advancement in the company. He had initially experienced an anxiety attack while conducting a sales meeting in a South American city that had particular emotional significance for him. (His young daughter had become seriously ill while the family was living in this city, necessitating an immediate return to the states to obtain adequate medical care.) Unable to complete his presentation, he excused himself and sought medical assistance. Returning the next day to New York, he consulted various specialists, but none could find a physical explanation for his experience. After several years of suffering, he was referred for psychiatric help. By this time he was using Valium daily but was getting relatively little relief for his anxiety.

After several sessions that included both relaxation training and discussion, Leon and I worked out a hierarchy of anxiety-producing situations and began desensitization. At the beginning, he felt very anxious if he was called into the office of a superior to explain a project or detail travel plans (he frequently traveled to South America), and was extremely intimidated by business dealings with others whom he considered of higher status than himself. Leon had been born in the Middle East and spoke with a pronounced, but very attractive, accent. He considered himself at a disadvantage, especially in dealing with foreigners, because, with his foreign accent and somewhat foreign appearance, he did not appear (and wasn't) the typical American businessman.

In addition to desensitization and assertive training, I suggested that Leon practice Transcendental Meditation. He did so and found the twice-daily meditation sessions to be of considerable benefit.

Although Leon's treatment required more than six months of weekly sessions, he gradually learned to handle increasingly difficult situations with less anxiety and less need for medication. By the end of the six months he had increased his international travel and was making sales presentations without much discomfort (and with little medication). He felt more optimistic about his chances for advancement, and his self-image was greatly improved.

It is very easy, especially for a shy person, to feel intimidated in interactions with superiors, even in relatively informal situations. When my oldest daughter, in her first job as an architect, was asked by her boss to stop by his office for a few minutes, she immediately wondered if she was going to be reprimanded for taking a legitimate sick day the day before. What he wanted to discuss, instead, was the fact that he would like her to start doing the firm's presentation drawings.

I cannot give a blueprint, or even write a script for you to use in practicing conversations with your boss—because every situation is so different—but *you* can. Make a list of the kinds of situations you find anxiety-provoking and create your own scripts for them. These could include such scenes as having a cup of coffee or lunch with your boss, explaining your department's projected sales campaign to your immediate superior, and making a presentation to a district sales office.

Making business presentations is only one step from formal speaking—and that, as noted before, is a problem for many people, even those who don't consider themselves especially shy. The way to get over your fear of presentations is to relax and imagine them—over and over if necessary—and to practice. The chances are you will be feeling much more relaxed by the twentieth presentation. A tape recorder may be helpful. Of course, for a business presentation, as for a formal speech, you must be well prepared. Few successful speakers (such as top executives) will make a formal presentation without writing it out in advance, though this is often not apparent from their delivery.

Finally, there is one other possible aspect which you may want to consider. In some cases (certainly not all) there are some concrete deficiencies that realistically add to your anxieties about public speaking. Have you analyzed your performance from this point of view? Leon, the sales engineer I mentioned, felt that his command of written English, while adequate by most standards, lacked the polish of a native speaker. I recommended that he obtain a tutor to help improve his writing skills. I referred a black woman who had risen to a supervisory position and felt inadequate about her spoken English to a speech therapist, because she was correct in feeling she needed help in this area. And I suggested that an aspiring woman executive who felt ill at ease about her appearance seek out a fashion consultant to give her the self-confidence that comes from knowing you are well dressed and look your best.

ACT I. HIRING LINE

SCENE 1. Telephoning for an appointment about a specific job

>VOICE: Good morning. Alpine Associates.
>
>YOU: My name is Carol Langsley. I'm calling about the position you advertised in today's paper.
>
>VOICE: Just a minute please, I'll connect you to Mr. Evan's office.
>
>YOU: Thank you.
>
>SECOND VOICE: Hello, Mr. Evan's office.
>
>YOU: My name is Carol Langsley. I'm calling about the position you advertised in today's paper.
>
>VOICE: We're interviewing experienced people only. Have you had any bookkeeping experience?
>
>YOU: Yes, I've been doing bookkeeping for the past five years, and am now working as head bookkeeper for Eagle Enterprises.
>
>VOICE: In that case I'd like to set up an appointment for you with Mr. Evan. Can you be here at nine tomorrow?
>
>YOU: Yes, I'll be there.

SCENE 2. Visiting an employment agency

>YOU: Hello. My name is Sara Smith. I'd like to talk to you about editorial jobs.
>
>COUNSELOR: Hello, Ms. Smith, I'm Joan Rawlings. Have you filled out our application?
>
>YOU: Yes, and I have a résumé and samples also.
>
>COUNSELOR: Let's see. It seems you've had a lot of experience, but you've been out of the job market for a while. Why is that?

YOU: I have two children and have been taking care of them. But they're both in school now and I am ready to go back to work.

COUNSELOR: What are you looking for in the way of salary?

YOU: I'd like to start at around $——.

COUNSELOR: That may be a little high for this area, but we do have a few jobs that might be appropriate. Let me make some calls and see if I can arrange some interviews. Are you free to go any time?

YOU: Yes. And the sooner the better!

SCENE 3. Telephoning for an appointment—with no specific job in mind

VOICE: Good morning. Intercontinental Company.

YOU: Mr. Anderson's office, please.

VOICE: Just a minute, I'll connect you.

YOU: Thank you.

SECOND VOICE: Mr. Anderson's office.

YOU: May I speak to Mr. Anderson, please?

VOICE: Who is calling?

YOU: My name is Bob Jansen. I'm calling at the suggestion of Ed Alpert, a friend of Mr. Anderson's.

VOICE: Just a minute, I'll see if he's available.

YOU: Thank you.

VOICE: Joe Anderson.

YOU: Mr. Anderson, my name is Bob Jansen. Ed Alpert suggested I call you. I'm a newspaper reporter with the *Post* and am thinking of making a career change. I'd appreciate it if I could come in and talk to you about the publicity business in general, and about the Intercontinental Company in particular.

VOICE: We don't have any openings right now, but I'll be happy to give you any information I can. Would next Wednesday at three be convenient?

YOU: That will be fine. Thank you so much, Mr. Anderson. I'll look forward to seeing you Wednesday at three.

POSTSCRIPT: After the meeting, a thank-you note is in order, and happens so infrequently that it will make a special impression.

Mr. Joseph Anderson
Publicity Manager
The Intercontinental Company
1234 5th Avenue
New York, N.Y. 10000

Dear Mr. Anderson:

I want to thank you for taking the time to meet with me yesterday. Your advice and counsel were most helpful.
   As soon as I have had the opportunity to follow up on your suggestions, I will call you.

Sincerely,

Bob Jansen

SCENE 4. Announcing yourself to the receptionist

The lobby of a modern office building. You have just arrived for your appointment with Mr. Howard.

RECEPTIONIST: Good morning. Can I help you?

YOU: I'm Don Berry. Mr. Howard is expecting me at ten.

RECEPTIONIST: Please have a seat. I'll tell Mr. Howard you are here.

YOU: Thank you.

RECEPTIONIST: Mr. Howard will be with you in just a few minutes.

SCENE 5. Having a job interview

The lobby of a modern office building. A tall, well-dressed man with a definite executive bearing enters the room and approaches you, extending his hand.

HE: Mr. Berry? I'm Jim Howard.

YOU: [Shaking hands]: Don Berry.

HE: My office is down this way. Follow me!

YOU: This is a handsome building. The firm hasn't been here long, has it?

HE: Only since October. Here we are. Why don't you take that comfortable chair over there?

YOU: Thank you.

HE: Let's see, I have your letter right here. You have an impressive background, and I like your work. What makes you think you'd like to work for *The Monthly Review?*

YOU: It's a magazine I've read regularly for years, and I've enjoyed every issue. I feel my own point of view, politically and philosophically, is compatible with the magazine's editorial stance. And it's important to me to work for something I can believe in.

NOTE: You'll have to take it from here and write your own script for each job interview. Consider questions you are likely to be asked and compose answers to them which present you favorably. Imagine comments and questions you can initiate that will indicate your interest in and knowledge of the company, and if possible the individual who is interviewing you. If the person interviewing you is well known, *Who's Who in America* or some other biographical dictionary can provide capsule information. Many firms publish annual reports and other brochures that can be obtained ahead of time. Never go unprepared to an important interview. You've worked hard to set up the interview; don't let yourself down at this important point.

A thank-you note, reaffirming your interest, is strongly recommended.

Mr. Don Berry
Editor-in-Chief
The Monthly Review
6000 Fifth Avenue
New York, N.Y. 10000

Dear Mr. Berry:

I certainly enjoyed our meeting yesterday and want to let you know again how much I would like to be a part of *The Review*. If there is any further information you need to assist you in making your decision, please call.

Sincerely,

Jim Howard

ACT II. NUTS AND BOLTS

SCENE 1. Explaining that you can't stay late

This is a situation that must be evaluated carefully. If you have a responsible job at the management level, you will be working late on some occasions by your own choice, just to get the job done. If your boss asks you to stay late to help out once in a while, you should do so if you can—otherwise, you're not going to get ahead. But if you have a personal engagement you can't conveniently break or don't want to break, or if you are constantly being taken advantage of and not reimbursed accordingly, you need to speak up.

HE: We have a lot of work to finish up tonight, Betty. I'm afraid I'm going to have to ask you to stay late again. We should be finished by eight.

YOU: I'm sorry, Mr. Jones, but this time I won't be able to help you out. I have other plans for this evening.

HE: You know how important this work is.

YOU: I'm sorry. If I had known about it earlier, in the day, perhaps I could have made some arrangements. But at this point, there is no way I can change my plans.

HE: I guess it can wait until tomorrow.

SCENE 2. Discussing your salary review with your boss

You have just been informed during your salary review that you have been given a smaller raise than you expected.

YOU: Mr. Jones, I don't understand why this raise is a smaller one than I had expected.

HE: It was felt that you weren't showing sufficient initiative on the job.

YOU: That must mean *you* feel I don't show initiative on the job, Mr. Jones. Could you explain exactly what that means?

HE: I'd like for you to go ahead and do things on your own, without waiting for me to tell you to do them.

YOU: When I have tried to do that in the past, Mr. Jones, I've always had the impression that you would prefer me to wait for your instructions. I'd appreciate it if you would let me know exactly what kinds of things you want me to do on my own.

HE: I'm going to give this some careful thought, Betty, and talk to you again in a day or two when I can give you some more specific suggestions.

YOU: Thank you.

SCENE 3. Asking for a raise

You have been working for six months on your first job as an architect. During that time you've been given increasing responsibilities, including designing and the preparation of presentation drawings. You are clearly being given more work than the other junior architects.

YOU: Ted, I'd like to talk to you about my salary.

HE: All right, Joe—talk!

YOU: It's been six months now since I came to work here, and I feel that I've been doing a very good job. I know I'm turning out a lot of work, and as far as I can tell everyone is pleased with what I'm doing.

HE: You're absolutely right. We're very happy with your work.

YOU: I'd like to have a raise, Ted. I don't feel that $—— is reasonable compensation for the job I'm doing.

HE: I'm inclined to agree with you. I'll see what I can do about getting you a raise to $——.

YOU: Ted, I would like to have $——.

HE: That sounds a little steep to me. Let me think it over and talk to Sam. I'll get back to you in a few days.

YOU: Thanks, Ted.

NOTE: When asking for a raise, the important issue is that your work merits it—not that you need it because the cost of living has gone up, because you have to buy a new car or your wife is sick. If you are doing a very good job and are convinced of that yourself, the chances are that you deserve a raise and can get one.

ACT III. PEOPLE PROBLEMS

SCENE 1. Asking a secretary to type a letter for you

A secretary's desk. You share this secretary with several other social workers at the clinic where you work.

YOU: Ginny, could you come into my office when you're free? I have a letter I'd like to dictate.

SHE: I can do it right now if that's convenient.

YOU: This goes to Dr. John Wright, New York Hospital, Bloomingdale Road, White Plains. Dear Dr. Wright. . . .

SCENE 2. Asking a secretary to retype a letter

A secretary's desk, as above.

YOU: Ginny, I'm going to have to ask you to retype this letter.

SHE: Why? What's wrong? I made a couple of mistakes, but I corrected them.

YOU: That's the problem. Corrections are fine if they don't show, but the appearance of this letter doesn't satisfy me.

SHE: I thought it looked all right.

YOU: I don't want to send it out over my signature like this. Please do it again.

SHE: I'll do it right away.

YOU: Thank you.

SCENE 3. Speaking to a subordinate about some unsatisfactory aspect of her performance

You have noticed that your new secretary spends a lot of time conducting personal conversations during business hours, and want to put a stop to it.

YOU: Joan, I want to talk to you about your personal telephone calls. Please don't make them from the office during business hours.

SHE: But I've only done that a few times, when something important has come up! At my last job, personal calls weren't a problem at all.

YOU: I'm afraid that it will be a problem here if it continues. Of course, if there is a genuine emergency, you are free to make any necessary call. And it isn't a problem if you call someone to arrange lunch, or they call you. I'm referring to the calls where you are having a long, friendly conversation with someone.

SHE: I'll be more careful in the future.

SCENE 4. Making a justified complaint to a colleague

You are a music teacher working as a team with another teacher. You have noticed that he frequently interrupts you when you are talking and that he seldom allows you to carry through with a topic you have introduced. This is becoming very annoying to you and you want to point it out to him.

YOU: Jim, it bothers me when you interrupt me in class. I feel like it undermines my authority with the students, and I don't like it.

HE: Oh, do I really do that?

YOU: Yes, you did it today when I started a discussion of the Pops concert on Sunday. You jumped right in and took over.

HE: You're right. I guess I did. I'm sorry, Nancy. I don't do that often, do I?

YOU: Yes, you do!

HE: I'm sorry. Let me know if I do it again.

YOU: Okay, I will.

SCENE 5. Asking a colleague to refrain from insulting you

You are a bank teller who has just been transferred to a different branch. The manager there has a heavy-handed manner in dealing with subordinates, and during the past week he has made several insulting remarks to you that were intended to be funny, but weren't. After thinking it over, you decide to speak up.

HE: Navy blue today! What do you think this is, police headquarters?

YOU: Mr. Williams, if you have some complaint about my work, I would like to know about it. But I don't like the personal remarks you have been making, and I'd appreciate it if you wouldn't do it.

HE: You're too sensitive.

YOU: You may feel that way, but I think your remarks are very insensitive, and I find them offensive

HE: I'm sorry. I shouldn't have said what I did.

ACT IV. ON THE FLOOR

SCENE 1. Speaking up in a meeting to disagree with a colleague.

A conference room. You are a middle management person in a large corporation. You are at a meeting of other department heads, where plans for the coming year are being reviewed. You don't agree with a point which has just been made by one of your colleagues.

HE: As I was saying, I think international travel should be restricted to forty days per year for any one employee.

YOU: I don't agree. There are times when that sort of regulation is self-defeating. I've just planned a trip to Colombia, for example, and it would make sense to stop in Mexico for several days on my way back. If I had a forty-day limit to contend with, that would adversely affect my planning.

HE: It's obvious in reviewing expense accounts that our employees are making travel plans without any consideration for the costs involved. If we set a maximum of forty days for international travel, we would get some control over this.

YOU: I just can't go along with that suggestion. It doesn't make good sense to me. We could suggest forty days as a guideline and let department heads make the final decision, since they have to approve travel plans anyway.

HE: We don't seem to be getting anywhere with this. I'm going to drop it for now, but I plan to draw up a memo on international travel to be presented at our next divisional meeting.

YOU: We can all give it some more thought in the meantime, but I for one am convinced that any specific limit would be a mistake.

SCENE 2. Defending a point or project when criticized by colleagues

A conference room. You have just presented an advertising budget for the next six months. You had expected this to be a routine presentation but are encountering some unexpected opposition from your colleagues.

HE: Joan, I think you're way out of line with your figures for TV spots. You can't justify such an expenditure.

YOU: I think I can. Customer survey figures indicate that our TV spots have been highly effective.

HE: That's a matter of interpretation. The same surveys show our magazine and newspaper ads have been highly effective too. And our dollars buy more exposure there.

YOU: That's also a matter of opinion. I feel certain it would be a mistake to reduce our TV budget when our competitors are pouring more and more into theirs.

HE: I don't think you've thought this through. I suggest you give it some further consideration.

YOU: I could do that, but it would just be delaying matters. I've recommended this advertising budget after careful consideration, and I don't plan to change my recommendation. I'd like to have a final decision today. Does anyone have any further comments before we vote on this?

Part **4**

POST
SCRIPTS

How to Meet 13 New People

The standard advice to people who want to meet other people is, I think, pretty good: Go where the kind of people you want to meet are likely to be, and be friendly when you get there.

Depending on where you live, there are many evening courses, special-interest groups, lectures, and other activities that will give you an opportunity to do something you enjoy and at the same time meet others with similar interests.

Do you like tennis? Check with tennis clubs in your area for information about clinics or round robins. Many clubs offer weekly mixed-double round robins. There are also possibilities for paddle tennis, squash, and racquetball. For people who like racquet sports, meeting others shouldn't prove too much of a problem.

Swimming? Try the YMCA. There are classes in swimming, water ballet, lifesaving, and scuba diving, plus scheduled "free swim" hours, and many communities have organized competitive events for all age groups through Masters Swimming.

Dancing? Arthur Murray or Fred Astaire may have the answer. Just because you've been sitting on the sidelines doesn't mean you have to stay there.

Drama? Join an amateur theater group. If you don't want to perform, you can paint scenery, help with lighting, or do publicity.

Birdwatching? The Audubon Club or your local nature center schedules lectures, field trips, and other special events.

Is painting, photography, or creative writing your thing? Many artists, both amateur and professional, find they are more productive and enjoy their work more if they spend some time learning and working with other artists. I recently rejoined a watercolor class myself, after years of not painting, and found it was just what I needed to get myself started again.

Whatever special interest you would like to pursue, one good place to begin looking is the adult education department of your local school system. In most communities, a wide range of courses are available at very low cost. In Norwalk, Connecticut, for example, the most recent brochure listed more than a hundred offerings, ranging from Italian conversation and cake decoration to auto mechanics and chair caning. And if there isn't enough to suit a Norwalk resident in Norwalk, he or she can go off a few miles to Stamford, pay a nonresident fee of two dollars, and choose from the even greater number of courses offered there.

Continuing education courses, not for credit, are also offered by many colleges and universities. Or perhaps you'd rather study for credit and work toward an undergraduate or graduate degree. Most colleges allow you to do so on a part-time basis.

The best source of information about what else is going on in your community is your local newspaper. Read it carefully and clip articles about activities of interest to you. (This is the procedure that works best for me, because if I don't clip an item out when I see it, I often can't find the page later or don't remember to go back and look.) Interesting lectures and discussions are often scheduled by libraries, churches, YMCAs and other institutions, and many of these events are free.

I urge clients who are trying to expand their social circles to attend at least one new event each week. After you start looking for places to go, you will be amazed at how many you can choose from.

Initially, when you are trying to break through the outer edges of your shyness, you may feel that it is easier to attend lectures and other special events if you can find a friend to go with you. If this is what it takes to get you going, do go with a friend the first few times. But as soon as you can bring yourself to do it, try going alone. You will find it easier to meet new friends if you don't have an old friend with you. Old friends are comfortable, and you can always talk to them without trying to branch out and meet others. But if you are all alone, you'll *have* to make the effort to walk up to strangers. They will be more likely to approach you, too, if you are alone. Women who travel in pairs are far less likely to have interesting adventures than those who strike out on their own.

There are interesting people everywhere, and I have never been in a group of people where there wasn't somebody I could enjoy talking to. In fact, I feel that I can enjoy talking to literally anyone for at least an hour and find every bit of the conversation interesting. (Granted, there are some I wouldn't care to spend a second hour with.)

If you have studied and rehearsed the scripts in earlier chapters for introducing yourself to others and getting conversations going, you should be able to enjoy yourself at any event you choose to attend. Remember it's only the first time, or the first few times, that will be difficult.

Of course I've had clients who got cold feet at the last minute and didn't actually get into the event, though they made it to the parking lot. The effect of this depends primarily on the way you look at it. You could regard it as a dismal failure and be very depressed by your inability to go through with it. Or you can take the positive approach—which is what I recommend—and say to yourself "This was a step in the right direction. This week I made it to the parking lot. Next week I'll go in." It actually is a kind of in vivo desensitization and in some cases, where clients are especially uptight about going someplace alone, this is the procedure I recommend.

You may discover, like one client of mine, that going with a friend will actually be more difficult than going alone, because you'll have to contend not only with your own apprehensions but with your friend's hangups also! Helen, an attractive divorced woman in her early thirties, finally persuaded herself to attend a singles discussion group at a local YMCA, but she didn't want to go alone and asked another divorced friend to go with her. But Helen's friend Beth was even more apprehensive than she was. They arrived in the lobby of the YMCA, whereupon Beth sat down on a bench and flatly refused to go in. Helen tried in vain to convince her that since they had come this far, they might as well go all the way. Not wanting to leave her friend sitting there, Helen eventually gave in and both of them left. The next week Helen went alone.

Which brings us to the issue of singles organizations and activities. If you are single or newly divorced, you can meet other people in the same situation through groups like Parents Without Partners and many other community-based or church-sponsored singles organizations. In some areas there are separate organizations for people of different age groups, for business and professional people, for widows and widowers, and so forth. Some of these organizations are so active that they literally have something going on every night of the week. There are also travel agencies specializing in tours and cruises for singles.

Singles bars are popular in some parts of the country. Your chances for meeting people you can be friends with, or form a serious relationship with, may not be great in a bar, but different people have different experiences, and expectations and customs vary widely from one part of the country to another. Singles bars for college students or young adults may have a different connotation than those for the older age groups. You can certainly find out by talking to others who have been there, or by going with a friend the first time to see what a certain place is like.

Dating services afford another possibility. A friend who is a magazine writer in New York says that "some of our staff have met terrific people through computer dating services." For a fee, these organizations attempt to match you up with members of the opposite sex who are appropriate in terms of educational background, interests, and personality. Some of these services have been very successful.

Some people look down on singles organizations, dating services, and other deliberate ways of meeting people, and wouldn't think of becoming involved. If you feel this way, that's your privilege, but it might be to your advantage to be a bit more open-minded.

One divorced man I met recently stated that he had

promised himself he would never attend a singles group or go to a singles bar—and he hadn't. He said that his philosophy about meeting people was that if you just went on doing your own thing, eventually something would turn up. But on the other hand, this same man's actions did not entirely fit with his statements. A tennis player suffering from tennis elbow, he had placed an ad in a local newspaper for "noncompetitive" players who would help him get his game back in shape. He received numerous calls, including one from me—that's how I met him. I admired his practical approach to problem-solving, and the experience made me wonder whether there aren't some other equally direct ways of meeting people.

A few days later I read an item in a newspaper about an "affluent" divorced Vancouver businessman in his forties who had placed a three-quarter-page ad in a Los Angeles paper for "a dream wife between 25 and 35, healthy, with good taste, beauty and a college education." Out of hundreds of replies, he selected twelve women for dinner dates, including a nurse, a home economist, a woman with an MBA, and another with a Ph.D. in English, but he didn't like any of the applicants.

I've also noticed ads in local papers for people who wanted to form singing groups, hoped to locate a guitarist for their rock band, get other agoraphobics together for a self-help group, or form a cooperative babysitting service. Make a habit of reading the "Personal" ads—or writing them'

There *are* creative solutions to problems if you have the imagination to see them. Writers, for example, can usually find ways of arranging interviews with people they want to meet. But if there's someone you'd like to meet and you don't happen to be a writer, you can find a way of being in the right place at the right time—casually. I happen to feel that there is at least one answer to every problem. And usually there are several.

After all this, there remains the possibility that you will meet exactly the person you have been looking for sitting (or standing) in a good friend's living room. I'm sure of it because it has happened—to me.

How to Make 14 Yourself a Better Conversationalist

There are two major elements in every conversation: you and the person you are talking to.

If you are carrying on a monologue, it may be very entertaining (it's more likely to bore your audience if it goes on too long, though) but it is not a conversation. That isn't to say that at times you shouldn't be the center of attention while you relate an interesting episode or experience.

But most shy people don't complain of delivering monologues or boring people with lengthy anecdotes. Their complaint is usually just the opposite: they have too little to say. This is why shy people frequently concentrate on being "good listeners." They're actually terrified that the other person will stop talking and *they'll* have to say something. If a person is a complete egomaniac, he or she may enjoy having a captive audience that doesn't provide any interference—

for a while. Eventually almost everybody gets bored with this kind of one-sided situation.

So I am not going to urge you to improve your conversational abilities by becoming a better listener. Some people could definitely profit from this advice, but most of them aren't shy. In a close relationship, of course, it's vitally important for both people to know how to listen as well as talk and to be able to communicate their understanding of the other's concerns and feelings. This is, however, a separate topic and one not especially related to shyness.

When I refer to improving your conversational ability, I'm thinking more specifically of ways you can help yourself have more interesting things to say and have more interesting exchanges of ideas with others.

I've already suggested that two basic rules for good conversation are: first, Don't ask any questions that can be answered merely yes or no, and second, Don't *answer* any questions with yes or no. If someone asks you if you liked a play, book, or movie, tell them *why* you did or didn't like it. You can go far on this rule alone.

When you are meeting people for the first time, you know little or nothing about them—and so there is everything to find out. You could carry on a rapid-fire interrogation, but this wouldn't be very satisfactory as a conversation. You must make sure you express some of your own personality too.

One of my young clients, meeting her college roommate-to-be a few weeks before the opening of school, felt very frustrated afterward because she had asked many questions, and received many answers, about the other girl's family, her high school experiences and her plans for the future—without having a chance to reciprocate. She felt that the roommate wasn't interested at all in her, since she had shown no interest and asked no questions. If you're not asked anything about yourself in such a situation, try to find a way of breaking into the flow of conversation occasionally to get in a few comments of your own. Don't just ask questions; make some statements, too.

One of my shy clients, a recent college graduate, came up with a good suggestion for sharpening conversational skills, which I'll pass along to you: Watch television interviewers and learn from them. You'll certainly get some ideas about ways of phrasing questions and comments which keep things moving along smoothly. (And you'll realize that these interviewers, or their staffs, do their homework ahead of time and have their questions prepared when their guest arrives.)

Make a habit of listening to dialogue in movies and plays. It's true that some of what you hear there would be unlikely to occur in real life, but that's mainly because the playwright or script writer has had the time to think over the situation and come up with the perfect response. The perfect response comes to most of us several days later, if at all.

You can also observe good conversationalists of your acquaintance and note what they talk about and how they keep things moving. Of course you won't have a great deal of time for observation since from now on you will be doing more talking yourself.

All of this adds up to the fact that you can learn something about the art of conversation by observing people who are good at it, just as you can learn something about tennis by watching Jimmy Connors or Chris Evert. (But it doesn't take a tennis player to know that you won't develop much of a game if all you do is watch other people play.)

What is it, exactly, that you learn from observations (and from putting these observations into practice)? You learn the *techniques* of conversation: ways of asking questions that will elicit interesting answers, ways of introducing your own comments and experiences naturally into the conversation, ways of making transitions from one topic to another, ways of introducing a totally new topic when the conversation comes to a standstill.

Each of these issues has already been touched on briefly, but I think they are worth reviewing.

How can you ask a question that will elicit an interesting answer? As you remember, you're going to phrase it so it cannot be answered merely yes or no. If you know anything at all about the person, or can deduce anything by looking at him or her, you can make some comment about that fact or observation, and follow it with a related question. For example: "I understand that you work with handicapped children. What do you feel is the most challenging case you have ever come across?" Or "Jane tells me you have been living in Mexico for the past five years. What has been the most difficult adjustment to make in coming back to the States?" Or "I was so interested in what you said about your method of raising tomatoes. Could you explain it to me more fully?"

How can you get something of yourself into the conversation when you seem to be the recipient of an ongoing monologue? Of course you aren't going to break into the middle of someone else's dramatic recital to clamor for attention yourself. You may want to draw out that person further about his or her experience. But let's assume that either the monologue has gone on too long, or merely long enough, and that you want to say something and have something to say.

There are a number of standard phrases which you should integrate into your repertoire. Memorize them if necessary; you will find them very useful in introducing an experience of your own. Here they are:

"I know exactly what you mean."

"I can imagine how you felt!"

"I had a similar experience recently myself."

"That reminds me of something which happened to me."

"What you just said reminds me of an experience of my own."

There are endless variations on this theme, but these suggestions should give you the idea.

How do you make transitions from one topic to another without giving the impression that you are hopelessly adrift (even if you are)? Similar phrases to those just enumerated can be used:

"Your comment raises the issue of . . ."

"That makes me wonder what you would think about the question of . . ."

"That reminds me of another problem I've been thinking about lately . . ."

At times, it may be desirable to close off a topic that is either getting too heated or too personal, or one that has merely been exhausted. You can often handle this directly by saying:

"It doesn't look as if we can resolve this problem tonight. I've been wondering what you think about . . ."

Or "I'd like to change the subject and go back to something we touched on earlier."

Or "Maybe we should let this topic simmer down for a while. I've been hoping for an opportunity to talk to you about . . ."

What if you are suddenly confronted with one of those dead spots in the conversation where nobody

is saying anything and the silence is getting more and more oppressive? I suggest that any time you anticipate being in a situation where this might happen, you prepare yourself ahead of time by making a list of possible topics (making a mental list may suffice, but if you are really uptight, writing it out and memorizing it will help).

Such topics mainly come under two categories: first, interesting experiences you have had and second, thoughtful or topical questions which can be used to provoke an interesting discussion.

The first category may simply be introduced by saying "I had the most interesting experience recently" or "The most surprising thing happened to me the other day" and then proceeding to describe your adventure, whatever it was. It's a good idea to think of some question you can add at the end of your anecdote, in case no one comes up with a spontaneous comment to keep the ball rolling. The question might be "Has anything like that ever happened to you?" or "How would *you* feel in a situation like that?"

A young woman in one of my shyness groups was going with her husband to a social function she dreaded. She had, the week before, obtained tickets to the King Tut exhibit by taking her place in line, along with a friend, at 6:30 A.M. She planned to keep her account of her early-morning vigil ready in case of a conversational emergency.

She also thought ahead to some questions she might bring up for general discussion. The group consisted of corporation executives and their wives, all of whom had presumably been transferred several times during their careers. Some of the possibilities Eloise came up with were: "I'll bet everyone in this room has moved at least five times. What do you consider your most difficult move?" and "Between us, we must have accumulated a lot of information about the art of getting settled into a new community. If a young couple being transferred to another part of the country asked you for advice, what would you say?" and "Hasn't it been inconvenient to be without *The New York Times* for two months? What do you miss most about the Sunday *Times?*" (This social event occurred during the 1978 New York newspaper strike.)

If you give a little advance thought to the person or persons you will be talking with, you can easily come up with a number of interesting topics. You'll find that the time you spend in preparation will pay off in making your conversations more interesting and in making you feel more at ease.

So much for technique.

There's also the question of content: having something to talk *about*. I firmly believe that every adult has things to talk about, whatever his or her life has been like. It is the way you view your life and your powers of observation and your sense of humor, among other factors, that determine what you can make of everyday experience.

I attended a professional conference recently at which one of the major speakers, a prominent psychologist beginning a new project on child abuse, introduced his topic by saying "My real question about this is not why it happens, but why it doesn't happen more often." He explained his statement by giving a humorous description of an evening spent trying to get his four children, aged two to ten, to bed by a certain hour so he could watch a television broadcast. The various domestic crises he enumerated were familiar to all parents, but his way of relating them raised an ordinarily frustrating experience to the level of entertainment.

As we all know, Jean Kerr and Erma Bombeck have both acquired fame and fortune by relating just such episodes in their own inimitable fashions. The experience is less important than the way you tell it. I might add parenthetically that you don't always have to tell it exactly like it is—artistic license allows you to exaggerate here and there if that helps your story, as long as your exaggeration is not at someone else's expense.

Before you say "Nothing ever happens to me," just stop and *think*. When people in my groups inform me that nothing happened this week, I feel almost certain they just didn't notice. Start noticing. And before you say "Things happen, but when I talk about them, they aren't interesting," give yourself a chance. Who says they aren't interesting? If you haven't told anybody about them, how do you know?

Some people have had fascinating experiences during their lifetimes, yet don't readily reveal them. While role-playing a scene in which a young divorced woman attended a singles "drop-in" party (about which she felt very apprehensive), I asked her what kind of leisure activities interested her most. When she replied that she loved to travel, I inquired about the most interesting place she had visited in the past year or so. She said, "That's hard to say I spent a week sailing around Nantucket, flew to Las Vegas for a weekend, where I won a thousand dollars, which enabled me to go on a show tour of London." This comment left me and the group members temporarily speechless. When we recovered, we all had many questions to ask her about her experiences. And she had thought she had nothing to say!

Take stock of your own experiences and decide which of them would be most interesting to others. And then keep them "on tap." If you had a Hollywood tryout at age five, people would like to hear about it. If you were on the *Today* show, everybody you meet would like to know what Jane Pauley was really like. (I'm sure the members of my first Shyness Clinic are still talking about that experience, and so am I.) If you once took a course in belly dancing, you can bet that will be good for a few minutes' animated conversation with almost anyone (granted there might be times when you wouldn't want to bring it up). If you went on an Outward Bound trip at sixteen, that's something almost everybody could relate to. Maybe you haven't done any of these exact things. But you have done *something*.

There's no doubt that some people have more interesting experiences, and have them more often, than other people. Why? Part of it is by chance, but not all. Not long ago I heard a very interesting and entertaining speech by Ann Landers, in which she divided people into three groups: those who make things happen, those who watch things happen, and those who say "What happened?"

You can learn to make things happen by enlarging the sphere of your own activities. Go to new places, do new things and meet new people, and things will start happening for you. Try a new sport, join a new club, and attend lectures and special events that interest you. This will serve the dual purpose of helping you meet new people and of helping you grow as a person.

Obviously, if you are going to make an intelligent contribution, or even any contribution, to conversations involving politics, current events, recent books or movies, or other topical matters, you must keep yourself informed about what is going on in the world.

I suggest that *everyone who wants to be well-informed* should read a daily newspaper. If you live in the New York area it should be *The New York Times* (plus, of course, any others you care to read). Take the weekly news quiz and work on improving your performance. If you live in another metropolitan area, read one of the leading newspapers in that city. If you live in a suburban or rural area, read the major metropolitan paper nearest you *and* read the daily or weekly paper published in your town. This is the only way to keep abreast of local happenings.

I find that many women do not read a newspaper. They feel inept, self-conscious, and "out of it" when they find themselves in a discussion of current topics. Occasionally I find myself in this position. There is only one way to remedy such a situation: read the paper.

Watching TV news or listening to radio broadcasts while driving or working will help, but this does not eliminate the need to read a daily newspaper. *Time* or *Newsweek* can also help you get it all together. Another good source of current conversational material is *People* magazine, which is easy and interesting to read.

You should try to keep informed about major events even if you aren't especially interested. If the U.S. Open is being played this week, make it your business to know who's playing. And don't neglect the theater, movie, and book reviews.

In addition, you should see some of the new movies and popular TV shows, and read the books that everybody is talking about. You can't read everything, but you should have some firsthand opinions about something. And when you read a book or see a play or movie, give some thought to it. Do you like it? Why? What do you like about it? Can you give an example of this? When I am working with people to improve their conversational skills, I have them practice asking themselves questions like these . . . and answering them.

Few people can be really interesting in a vacuum. Do interesting things yourself and read about interesting things and you will have interesting things to talk about.

As you feel yourself becoming more interested in the world around you, and simultaneously feel yourself becoming more interesting, you'll find that your shyness will bother you less and less. The more self-confident you feel, the more at ease you will be in social situations. It isn't a change which is going to occur overnight or even in a matter of a few weeks, especially if your shyness problem is one which has been with you a long time. The important thing to remember is that you *can* overcome your shyness. And if you follow the suggestions I have given you, I know you *will* overcome it. Many people have already done so. So can you.

INDEX

in classroom, 121–123
in social situationss, 125–129

Headaches, 34
High blood pressure, 34
How to Talk with Practically Anybody about Practically Anything (Walters), 133, 134

Insomnia, 34
Interviews for jobs, 154–160, 168–169
Introductions
  introducing others, 80–89
    two strangers, 80–81, 88
    when you forget a name, 88–89
  introducing yourself, 55–74
    to another member of small group at first meeting, 58
    in business situation, opposite sex, 61
    in business situation, same sex, 60–61
    to classmate, opposite sex, 59–60
    to classmate, same sex, 58–59
    exchanging names with acquaintance, 73
    exchanging names with someone new, 73–74
    reintroducing yourself in casual situation, 70
    reintroducing yourself in social situation, 70–71

reintroducing yourself to someone from past, 71–72
reintroducing yourself to someone who doesn't remember you, 72
reintroducing yourself to someone whose name you've forgotten, 72
at singles party, opposite sex, 64–65
at singles party, same sex, 63–64
at singles party, to two or more, 67–68
in small group as part of routine first night procedure, 65
in social situation, opposite sex, 63
in social situation, same sex, 61–63
in social situation, to two or more, mixed group, 66–67
in social situation, to two or more, same sex, 65–66
in vacation setting, to two or more, 68–69
Inviting, 101–117
See also Dating

Jacobson, Edmund, 34
Jameson, R. J., 153

About the Author

Barbara Powell, Ph.D., is a clinical psychologist practicing in Rowayton, Connecticut. In addition to working with individuals, she conducts assertiveness training programs, shyness clinics, and groups for phobic patients. She is the author of *How to Raise a Successful Daughter*, and *Careers for Women after Marriage and Children*.

Catalog

If you are interested in a list of fine Paperback
books, covering a wide range of subjects
and interests, send your name and address,
requesting your free catalog, to:

McGraw-Hill Paperbacks
1221 Avenue of Americas
New York, N.Y. 10020